Grade 8

Addison-Wesley Mathematics

Challenges Workbook

▲▼ Addison-Wesley Publishing Company

Menlo Park, California ■ Reading, Massachusetts ■ New York
Don Mills, Ontario ■ Wokingham, England ■ Amsterdam ■ Bonn
Sydney ■ Singapore ■ Tokyo ■ Madrid ■ San Juan

ISBN 0-201-27811-1

ABCDEFGHIJKL-HC-96543210

Table of Contents

Name _____

Space Map

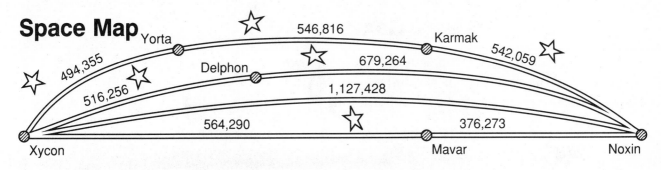

Yorta   546,816   Karmak   542,059

494,355   Delphon   679,264

516,256

1,127,428

564,290   376,273

Xycon   Mavar   Noxin

The space travelers using this map measure distances in termins.

1. A spaceship started at Delphon and traveled about 500,000 termins to a nearby planet. At which planet did it stop?

_____

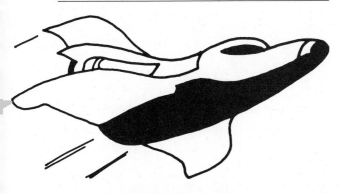

2. Between which two planets is the map distance 400,000 termins when rounded to the nearest hundred thousand?

_____

3. Which distance is farther, Yorta to Karmak or Karmak to Noxin?

_____

4. Between which planets is the map distance 500,000 termins rounded to the nearest hundred thousand?

_____

_____

_____

5. Between which two planets is the distance between 400,000 and 500,000 termins?

_____

6. The spaceships in this galaxy hold only enough fuel to travel 550,000 termins. Between which points on the map can a spaceship travel without refueling?

_____

_____

_____

_____

7. Between which two points is the distance 540,000 termins when rounded to the nearest ten thousand?

_____

8. List in order from least to greatest the distances between points on the map.

_____   _____

_____   _____

_____   _____

The "Same Answer" Game

Work in groups. Each of you should have your own calculator. Follow directions carefully.
Remember to press $=$ after each calculation.

1. —Enter your birthday. (Example: for March 23, enter "23.")

—Put this number in the memory.

—Add 5.

—Multiply by 2.

—Subtract 4.

—Divide by 2.

—Subtract the memory.

Answer: _____

Compare your answer with those of the other students in your group. Is it the same?

2. —Enter the number in your street address.

—Put this number in the memory.

—Multiply by 5.

—Subtract 7.

—Multiply by 4.

—Add 8.

—Divide by 20.

—Add 18.

—Subtract the memory.

Answer: _____

Compare your answer with those of the other students in your group. Is it the same?

3. —Enter your phone number.

—Put this number in the memory.

—Divide by 2.

—Add 9.

—Multiply by 10.

—Subtract the memory.

—Divide by 4.

—Subtract the memory.

Answer: _____

Compare your answer with those of the other students in your group. Is it the same?

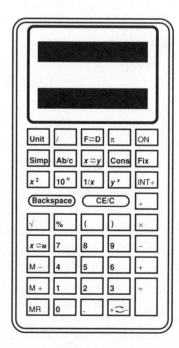

Name _____

Magic Multiplication Squares

In a magic multiplication square the product of the numbers in each row, column, and diagonal is the same. Use the given numbers to make the magic squares. Each square has more than one solution!

1. Use 2, 4, 8, 10, 40, 50, 100, and 200. The magic product is 8,000.

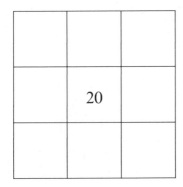

2. Use 1, 2, 4, 10, 40, 100, 200, and 400. The magic product is 8,000.

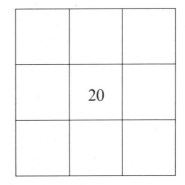

3. Use 5, 10, 20, 50, 200, 500, 1,000, and 2,000. The magic product is 1,000,000.

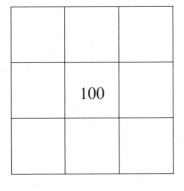

04. Use 20, 40, 80, 100, 400, 500, 1,000, and 2,000. The magic product is 8,000,000.

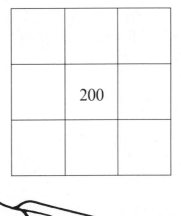

Triangle Mazes

Round each number to the nearest ten thousand. Write the rounded number in the triangle.

Then use estimation to trace a path through the triangles so that the numbers add up to the exit number.

1. 34,284

2. 76,266

3. 23,845

4. 69,124

5. 37,875

6. 18,115

7. 30,903

8. 76,543

9. 9,234

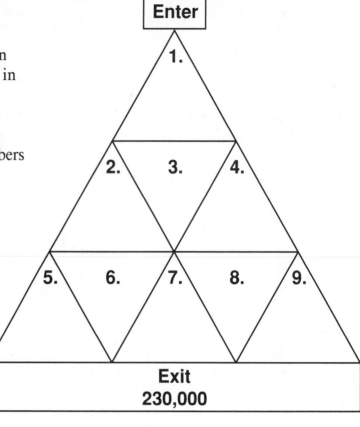

Round each number to the nearest hundred thousand. Write the rounded number in the triangle.

Then use estimation to trace a path through the triangles so that if you subtract the smaller number from the larger along the path, the final difference is the exit number.

1. 2,377,205

2. 724,057

3. 314,269

4. 918,573

5. 183,492

6. 642,135

7. 730,218

8. 474,333

9. 193,457

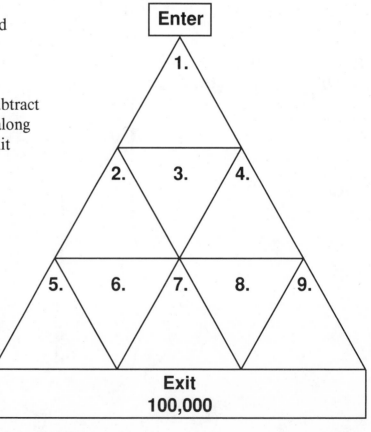

Name _____

Introduction

Write an equation that tells how to find the answer. Then use a calculator to find the result.

The Chore Company of Wytack manufactures large robots. Each type A robot requires 102 gears for assembly. Each gear requires 38 teeth. Each tooth requires 14 seconds to manufacture. The company makes 68 type A robots a day.

1. How many gears are needed each day?

_____

_____

2. How many teeth are used each day?

_____

_____

3. How many minutes are needed to manufacture all the teeth for 1 day?

_____

_____

4. There are 20 working days per month. In 1 year, how many type A robots are made?

_____

_____

The sale sign on the shoe store stated that all sneakers were reduced to $29.90, boots to $39.50, and slippers to $8.75.

5. During the sale, 16 pairs of boots, 5 pairs of slippers, and 19 pairs of sneakers were sold. What was the total income from the sale?

_____

_____

6. The net profit on each pair of boots or sneakers was $5.40. If 19 pairs of sneakers and 16 pairs of boots were sold, what was the net profit?

_____

_____

7. Could you buy 3 pairs of sneakers and 3 pairs of boots for under $100? Explain your answer.

_____

_____

8. After the sale, sneakers were increased by $11.25. In two weeks a dozen pairs of sneakers were sold. What was the income?

_____

_____

Name _____

Symmetric Multiplication

Joan discovered a new method for multiplying
certain pairs of numbers. Study her method.

```
      999
    × 222
       18
     1818
   181818
     1818
       18
   221,778
```

Check →
```
        999
      × 222
       1998
       1998
       1998
     221,778
```

Write these symmetrically.

```
         3,333
       × 4,444
            12
          1212
        121212
      12121212
        121212
          1212
            12
      14,811,852
```

Check →
```
         3,333
       × 4,444
         13332
         13332
         13332
         13332
       14,811,852
```

Use Joan's method to find these products. Check
your answer by multiplying the regular way.

1.
```
   222
 × 333
    06
  0606
```

2.
```
   666
 × 333
```

3.
```
   444
 × 888
```

4.
```
   777
 × 777
```

5.
```
   9,999
 × 4,444
```

6.
```
   6,666
 × 3,333
```

7.
```
   4,444
 × 2,222
```

8.
```
   8,888
 × 6,666
```

Basically the Same

The computer language BASIC (Beginner's
All-purpose Symbolic Instruction Code) uses
operation symbols that are similar to those in
mathematics.

Operation	Mathematics	BASIC
Add	$3 + 5$	$3 + 5$
Subtract	$8 - 7$	$8 - 7$
Multiply	$4 \times a$	$4 * A$
Divide	$20 \div 2$	$20/2$
Raise to a power	t^2	$T \uparrow 2$

The order of the operations is the same in BASIC
as in mathematics.

1. Do all operations within parentheses.
2. Evaluate all powers from left to right.
3. Do all multiplications and divisions from left to right.
4. Do all additions and subtractions from left to right.

Translate each of the following into BASIC. Then
solve each for $n = 8$.

1. $n \div 8$

_____

2. $6n + 4$

_____

3. n^3

_____

4. $(12 - n) \times 10$

_____

5. $72 \div n$

_____

6. $4 \times n - n$

_____

Translate each of the following into a mathematical
expression. Then solve each for $t = 5$.

7. $(T + 1) \uparrow 4$

_____

8. $T/6$

_____

9. $(3 * 4) \uparrow T$

_____

10. $6 * (4 + T)/9$

_____

11. $(T + 7)/(T - 2)$

_____

12. $T + (T/5 + 10)$

_____

4-Step Multiplication

Here is a way to multiply any two numbers that have the same tens digit.

Use the following steps:

► Add one number and the units digit of the other number.

► Multiply the result by the tens digit. (Remember: the tens digit is the same for both numbers.)

► Affix a 0.

► Multiply the units digits of the original two numbers and add the product to the number you got in step 3.

Example:

34×35

► $34 + 5 = 39$

► $39 \times 3 = 117$

► $1,170$

► $4 \times 5 = 20$; $1,170 + 20 = \mathbf{1,190}$

Example:

77×71

► $77 + 1 = 78$

► $78 \times 7 = 546$

► $5,460$

► $7 \times 1 = 7$; $5,460 + 7 = \mathbf{5,467}$

Use the 4-step rule to find each product. Check the answers with your calculator.

1. 61×69 **2.** 12×18 **3.** 89×89 **4.** 74×79

_____ _____ _____ _____

5. 83×87 **6.** 37×35 **7.** 48×46 **8.** 56×57

_____ _____ _____ _____

Guestimate Game

Play this estimation game with 6 or more people.
Each player needs paper and pencil.

1. Write one of the suggested questions below on
a card for each player and have each player
make a chart for recording answers.

Answers				
1. _____	2. _____	3. _____	4. _____	5. _____
Highest answer _____		Lowest answer _____		Average _____

2. Tape a question card onto the back of
each player without letting that player
see the question.

3. Players circulate reading all questions
silently except their own. They estimate
answers to all 5 other players questions
and give their estimates to the player
with the question on his or her back.

4. After getting answers, each player
records the highest and lowest answer
and computes the average answer.

5. Then one at a time each person reads his
or her question aloud and reports the
range and average answer. Knowing the
question, the players should pick a
sensible estimate together.

Suggested Questions (Make up your own for the next game.)

► How many hours of TV does
the average 8th grader watch in one year?
► About how many times a day does
the average American blink?
► About how many vitamin pills does
the average American take in 1 year?
► About how many miles long
is the line drawn by the average pencil?
► Approximately how many seconds
are there in a day?

► About how many times a day does
the average American laugh?
► About how many apples does
the average 8th grader eat in one year?
► About how many breaths does
the average person take in one day?
► About how many hours of homework
does the average 8th grader do in one
year?

Guessing a Birthday

Here is a way that you can guess your friends' birthdays!
Ask your friend to:

1. Multiply the month of his or her birth by 5.
(Suppose your friend's birthday is December 6: $12 \times 5 = 60$.)

2. Subtract 3.
$(60 - 3 = 57)$

3. Double the number.
$(57 \times 2 = 114)$

4. Multiply the number by 10.
$(114 \times 10 = 1,140)$

5. Add the day of birth.
$(1,140 + 6 = 1,146)$

Have your friend tell you this final number.
To guess your friend's birthday, add 60 to the
number.

$$(1,146 + 60 = 1,206)$$
12 06 is December 6.
↑ ↑
month day

The first two digits are the month and the last two digits are the day.

DECEMBER						
Sunday	Monday	Tuesday	Wednesday	Thursday	Friday	Saturday
					1	2
3	4	5	6	7	8	9
10	11	12		14	15	16
17	18	19	20	21	22	23
24/31	25	26	27	28	29	30

Use with text pages 22–23.

Name _____

Scrambled Numbers

Here are some sets of interesting data. The numbers
are all correct; however, they may have been placed
incorrectly. Use the clues to place each number
correctly.

1. Four of the world's tallest structures are the CN Tower in Toronto, Canada (1,353 ft),
the Sears Tower in Chicago (2,020 ft), the World Trade Center in New York (1,815 ft),
and the Warsaw, Poland, Radio Mast (1,454 ft).

▶ Only one structure is shorter than the Sears Tower.

▶ Only one structure is taller than the CN Tower.

▶ The World Trade Center is not the tallest structure.

Actual heights: CN Tower _____   World Trade Center _____

Sears Tower _____   Warsaw Radio Mast _____

2. The four largest islands in the world are New Guinea (316,856 mi), Borneo (840,000
mi^2), Madagascar (286,967 mi^2), and Greenland (227,000 mi^2).

▶ Borneo is almost exactly 60,000 mi^2 larger than the world's fourth largest island.

▶ Most of the world's largest island is covered with snow.

▶ New Guinea is the second largest island.

Actual sizes: New Guinea _____   Borneo _____

Madagascar _____   Greenland _____

3. The length of days (measured in Earth time) on four planets are: Mercury (10 hr
14 min), Saturn (243 da), Venus (6 da), and Pluto (59 das).

▶ A day on Venus is closest to the length of a year on Earth.

▶ A day on Mercury lasts almost ten times as long as a day on Pluto.

Actual lengths: Mercury _____   Saturn _____

Venus _____   Pluto _____

Name _____

Football Scores

These charts show football scores for games played by
the Hawks and by the Wildcats.

Hawks	17	14	21	17	7	3	28	10	20	14
Opponent	3	14	13	21	3	13	7	14	7	35

Wildcats	21	13	7	13	7	17	30	20
Opponent	17	3	7	10	28	13	14	21

1. Complete this chart using the data above.

Team	Games won	Games lost	Games tied	Games played
Hawks				
Wildcats				

2. Make circle graphs to show the number of games won,
lost, and tied for each team.

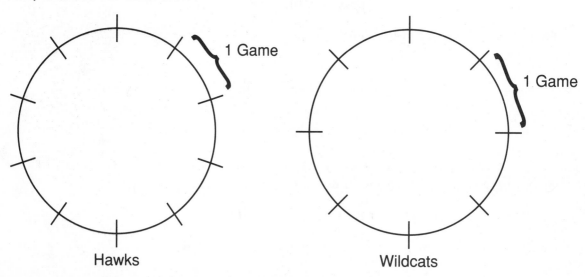

Hawks   Wildcats

1 Game   1 Game

3. Even though each team won 5 games, one team had a
better record. Which team?

_____

Classy Graphs

Choose from bar, circle, and line graphs. Tell which would *not* be appropriate to display the following data. Explain. Then sketch an appropriate graph.

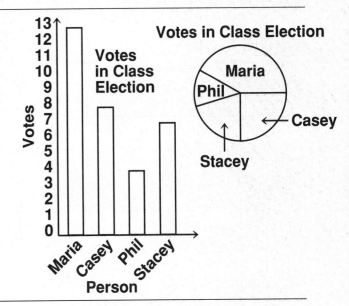

1. Class president election results

Maria	13
Casey	8
Phil	4
Stacey	7

Inappropriate: _____

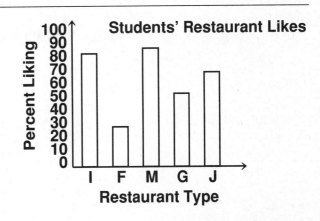

2. Percent of students in class who like the following kinds of restaurants

Italian	85%
French	30%
Mexican	89%
Greek	55%
Japanese	71%

Inappropriate: _____

---

3. The trend in video watching by the class for the month of November by weeks

Week 1	37
Week 2	45
Week 3	58
Week 4	42

Inappropriate: _____

Magic Rows

Follow these steps.

1. Pick any number from the chart.
   Cross out all other numbers in the same
   row and column of the number you chose.

2. Repeat step 1 until each column has only
   one number left.

3. Add these numbers.
   What is your answer? _____

4. Repeat steps 1 through 3 two more times.

   What are your answers? _____

Can you figure out why? What is the trick?

	21	**13**	**10**	**9**	**11**
0	21	13	10	9	11
1	22	14	11	10	12
3	24	16	13	12	14
15	36	28	25	24	26
2	23	15	12	11	13

Name _____

Best Guessing Game

> Dear Family,
> Here is a chance to do some research and have some fun. You can either work together or have a contest.

How well do you think you estimate?

Make a guess for each of these facts. Then look each one up in either an almanac or the Guiness Book of World Records. These books can be found at any library. Record the actual number and find the difference between it and your guess. When you finish, add the differences. If the sum is less than 60, you really know your facts! If the sum is greater than 60, you might want to read the two books more carefully. They're fascinating!

Fact	Guess	Actual	Difference
1. Number of members of the United Nations	____	____	____
2. Height in feet of Niagara Falls	____	____	____
3. Number of American cities with more than 1,000,000 people	____	____	____
4. Total number of American Presidents	____	____	____
5. Number of working nuclear power plants in the United States	____	____	____
6. Weight in pounds of the heaviest turkey	____	____	____
7. The circumference in feet of the world's largest ball of string	____	____	____

Do you think some of the records may change from year to year? _____

_____

Choose a Path

Copy this drawing without lifting your pencil and without retracing any lines. Write the path you traveled using the letters shown.

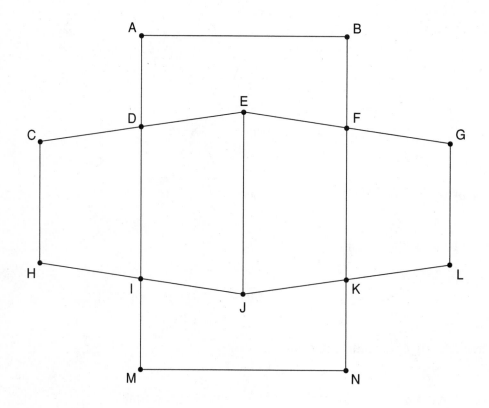

Name _____

Skate Data

Ginny said, "I paid a $10 membership fee. Now it only costs me $2 each time I skate. I have the best deal!"

"No way!" James claimed. "Although I pay $4 each time I skate, I did not pay the $10 membership fee. I have a better deal."

Who is right?

1. Complete the table.

Skate times	0	2	4	6	8	10	12
Member	$10						
Nonmember	0						

2. Plot the data from the table to show a line graph for members and another one for nonmembers. Label both.

3. How much will a nonmember pay to skate 14 times?

_____

4. How much will it cost for a member to skate 14 times?

_____

5. Who has the better deal if he or she wants to skate only 4 times?

_____

6. Who has the better deal if he or she wants to skate only 5 times?

_____

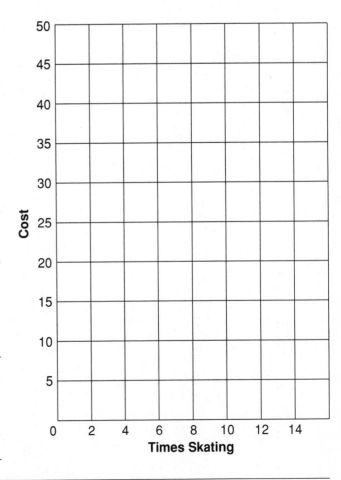

Spinners and Dice

1. What do you predict will be the mean value for one spin of this 8-section spinner?

_____

Use an 8-section spinner. Spin it 20 times. Write the results here.

____ ____ ____ ____

____ ____ ____ ____

____ ____ ____ ____

____ ____ ____ ____

____ ____ ____ ____

Now calculate.

Mean: _____

Median: _____

Mode: _____

Are these numbers close to your guess?

_____

2. What do you predict will be the average total for 6-sided number cube when you toss 5 number cubes at once?

_____

Ask your teacher for 5 dice. Throw the whole set of dice on your desk ten times. Write the ten totals here.

____ ____ ____ ____

____ ____ ____ ____

____ ____

Now calculate.

Mean: _____

Median: _____

Mode: _____

Are these numbers close to your guess?

_____

Target in Range

> Dear Family,
>   Calculators are an excellent tool for simplifying everyday arithmetic.
> They can also be used as part of many enjoyable mathematics games.

This game for two players will test your estimation skills.

Begin with the entry number. Multiply or divide by any number to get to the target. Do *not* clear the calculator following each step. A player continues until he or she reaches the target range. The winner is the player who reaches the target range using the fewest steps.

For example:

Entry Number	Target
17	9,350–9,450

First step: 17×500 8,500 (not within range)

Second step: $8,500 \times 1.4$ 11,900 (overshot the target)

Third step: $11,900 \div 1.27$ 9,370 (in range)

This round took 3 steps.

	Entry Number	Target
Game 1	6	725–750
Game 2	500	13–20
Game 3	23	22,000–22,100
Game 4	1,250	950–975
Game 5	1.7	85–90
Game 6	125,000	300–350

Significant Magic Figures

You have seen magic squares. Perhaps you have even
seen magic triangles. You can think of the numbers in
each figure as a set of data. The numbers added
horizontally, vertically, and diagonally give the
same sum.

In the magic figures shown here, the pattern does not
seem to work. For example, in the magic square,
$19.32 + 28.341 + 37.3$ *does not exactly equal*
$19.32 + 34.319 + 31.398$. However, you can turn
these into true magic figures by following these steps.

1. Copy the figures, but not the
numbers inside the boxes.

2. Find the entry in each figure
with the fewest number of significant
digits.

3. Round all other entries to the
number of significant digits from
step 2.

4. Fill in the blank squares to
complete each magic figure.

19.32	34.319	31.398
	28.341	
		37.3

What is the sum for the magic square? _____

The magic triangle? _____

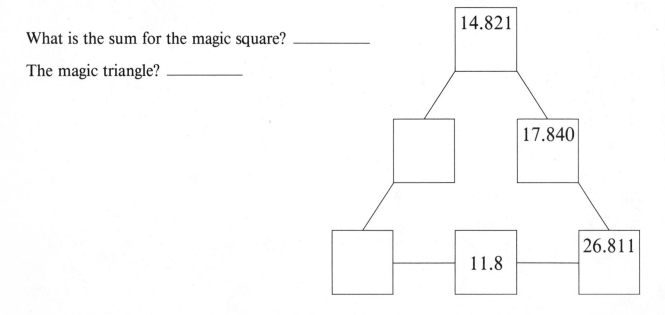

Zany Figures

Only the numbers have to be true in the stories below.
Fill in the number blanks so that the arithmetic is
correct. Fill in the other blanks however you wish.

1. Last year the _____
movie theater sold 272,378 adult tickets

and _____ child tickets.
number
They sold 463,042 tickets in all.

2. The biggest-selling movie last year was

_____, which ran for 5

weeks and sold _____
number
adult tickets and 13,591 child tickets.
In all, 52,004 tickets were sold for this
movie.

3. A rock group, the _____,
gave a concert last year to 5,264
people. This year their concert was

attended by _____ people,
number
which was an increase of 389 over last
year's attendance.

4. Mr. _____ won $65,000

last year in the _____
contest. He spent $15,768 of this on a

new car and $23,428 on a _____.

He has _____ left.
number

5. If I had a million dollars, I would give

$375,000 to _____,

$215,000 to _____,

$145,000 to _____, and
keep the rest myself. I would be keeping

_____ for myself.
number

6. My friend, _____, wrote

a book called _____. The

first year it sold 3,720 copies, the
second year 4,198 copies, and the third

year _____ copies. The
number
total number of copies sold in the three
years was 15,632.

7. Last year a store sold 64,821 _____.
This year the number sold was 3,762

less. This year only _____
number
were sold.

8. I can't wait to tell my friends that I

won 26,500 _____ in a

_____ contest. I'm giving

16,250 to _____ so I'll

only have _____ left.
number

Magic Number Patterns

Numbers form many fascinating patterns. Some of
these patterns enable you to do what appear to be
magic tricks. Of course, what makes the trick possible
is the way our number system is set up.

Here is an interesting trick to try. Follow the steps
yourself before trying it on someone else.

1. Select 3 **different** digits smaller than 10.

2. Make all the different 2-digit numbers you can
from the 3 digits. You should be able to make 6
different 2-digit numbers.

3. Add the 6 numbers.

4. Add the original 3 digits you selected.

5. Divide the sum from step 3 by the sum from step
4. For example, suppose you chose the digits 2, 7,
and 9. You can make these numbers: 27, 29, 72,
79, 92, and 97. If you add them, you get 396.

When you add the original digits, you get 18. Now

divide 396 by 18. What is the quotient? _____

Try these other sets of numbers: 1, 4, 8 and 3, 5, 7.

What is the quotient each time? _____

Do you see why this happens?

_____

_____

_____

_____

_____

_____

Now you are ready to "predict" the quotient for anyone else!

Estimating Area

Here is a chance to test your estimation skills on the concept of area.

Look at the square to the right. If you found the midpoint of each side and connected them in order, what type of polygon do you think would be formed? Try it and see.

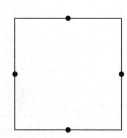

Estimate the relationship between the area of the original square and the polygon formed by connecting the midpoints of the sides.

You can check your estimate this way.

►Assume that the length of each side of the original square is 8 units.

►You can find the area of each right triangle:
Area of each triangle $= \frac{1}{2}bh = \frac{1}{2} \cdot 4 \cdot 4 = 8$ sq. units

►The total area of all 4 right triangles is 4×8 or 32 square units.

►You know the area of the original square:
$$8 \times 8 = 64 \text{ square units.}$$

►Therefore, the area of the small polygon must also be 32 square units or one half of the original square.

Follow the same steps for the rectangle shown here.

► What kind of polygon do you think will be formed?

► What is the area of the original rectangle?

► What is the area of the small polygon?

What generalizations do you think you can make:

► About the kind of polygon formed when you connect the midpoints of the sides of

any 4-sided polygon? _____

► About the size of the smaller polygon? 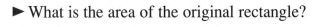 _____

Five-Piece Puzzles

Measure the five pieces below. Use the pieces to solve these two puzzles.

1. Arrange the five pieces to form two squares. One square is 6 cm on each side. The other is 8 cm on each side.

2. Arrange the five pieces to form one square. It will be 10 cm on each side.

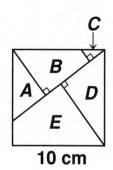

10 cm

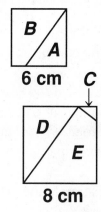

6 cm

8 cm

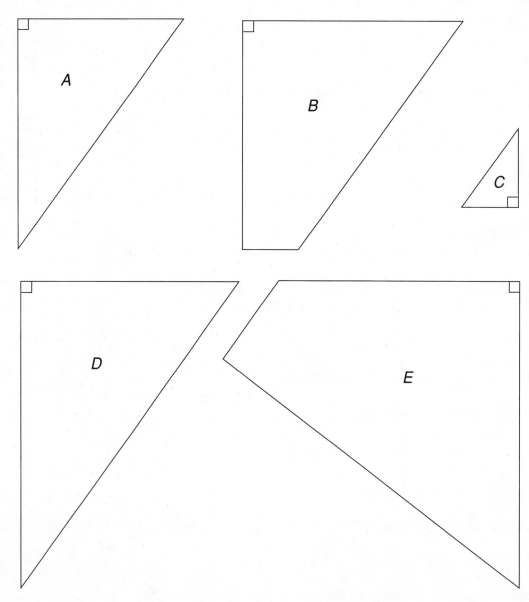

Problem Solving

Think creatively to solve these two problems.

1. Trace this circle onto a sheet of unlined paper. Without using a protractor, a ruler, a pencil, or any other tool, find the center point of the circle.

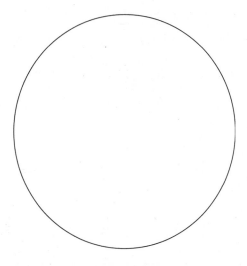

Explain how you found the center. _____

_____

_____

_____

2. Trace this arc onto a sheet of unlined paper. If it were continued, it would form a circle. Again, without using any tools, and without extending the arc, find the center of the circle of which this arc is part.

Explain what you did. _____

_____

_____

Frame Ups

Imagine that you work in a framing shop. When customers come in to place an order, your job is to draw a sketch, including all dimensions, of what they would like. Your boss also expects you to tell her how much framing material will be needed.

Here are some orders that were placed recently. For each one, draw a sketch with dimensions. Your sketch does not have to be exactly to scale; however, all customers would like their pictures centered in the frames. Then write the area of framing material that will be needed. All perimeter dimensions are in whole numbers.

1. A square frame with perimeter of 64 inches
A square picture with area of 64 square inches

Area of frame = _____

2. A trapezoidal frame with area of 100 square inches
A circular picture with diameter of 6 inches

Area of frame = _____

3. A rectangular frame with perimeter of 72 inches
A rectangular picture with area of 252 square inches

Area of frame = _____

4. A rectangular frame with area of 288 square inches
A square picture with perimeter of 32 inches
A circular picture with radius of 4 inches

Area of frame = _____

No Numbers

The numbers have been left out of these problems. Tell how you would solve each problem and what formulas you would use.

Pool ◁—Deck

1. Mr. and Mrs. Johnson are having their twenty-fifth wedding anniversary. They are putting silver braid around the border of a circular tablecloth that has a diameter of ☐ yd. The braid costs $ ☐ /yd. How much will it cost to trim the cloth?

    _____

    _____

2. The Barrys are building a deck around a circular pool in their backyard. The pool has a diameter of ☐ yd and the deck has a diameter of ☐ yd. How many square yards is the deck area not counting the pool?

    _____

    _____

3. Mr. and Mrs. Getty are insulating their attic. The attic has one rectangular area ☐ ft by ☐ ft and another rectangular area ☐ ft by ☐ ft. The insulation costs $ ☐ /ft². What will it cost to insulate the attic?

    _____

    _____

4. Larry is having a bedspread made for his room. The labor charge is $ ☐ /ft². The spread will cover the top of the bed, which is ☐ ft by ☐ ft, and will overhang ☐ ft on all four sides. What will be the cost of the labor?

    _____

    _____

5. Kay is getting ready to buy wallpaper for her room. She needs to calculate the area of the walls. The room is ☐ ft by ☐ ft with ☐ -ft-high ceilings. The total area of the door and two windows is ☐ ft². How many square feet of wall area are in the room?

    _____

    _____

6. Mary is having a shade made for her bedroom window. She needs ☐ yd of fabric at $ ☐ /yd. The window is ☐ ft by ☐ ft. The charge for labor is ☐ /ft². What is the total cost of the shade?

    _____

    _____

Space Perception

You can fold a square sheet of paper into a cube.
Dotted lines are folds.

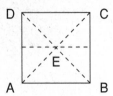

Fold a square sheet of paper
three times as shown.

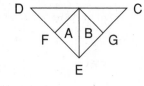

Make a triangular shape.

Fold points A and B down
to E.

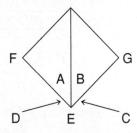

Fold points D and C down to
E, behind A and B.

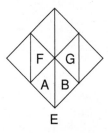

Fold the top corners inward at
F and G to the center line.

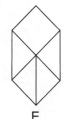

Fold the other two corners
backward to the center line on
the back.

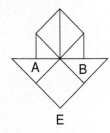

Fold back loose corners A and
B. Do the same for the loose
corners in the back.

Fold points A and B to the
center. Repeat for the points
in the back.

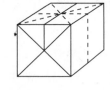

Tuck △AXY and △BRS into
the pockets under A and B.
Repeat for the triangles in the
back.

Fold points O and E to the
center and back again.

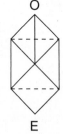

Blow in the hole at point O to
inflate the cube.

A paperfolded cube!

Name _____

Sea Search

Airplanes are often used in rescue missions to search for missing ships at sea. The planes follow circular paths like those below to be sure of covering the complete search area. The grid shows planes about to start flying their routes 50 miles apart.

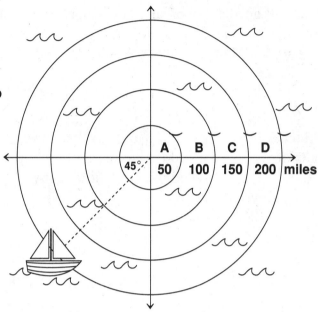

A calculator will be helpful to answer the questions. Use 3.14 as π.

1. How many square miles of ocean must plane A search?

_____

2. How many miles will plane B have traveled when it has made one complete revolution?

_____

3. What is the total area that the four planes must search?

_____

4. Plane B travels at 200 miles per hour. To the nearest hour, how long will it take to complete one revolution?

_____

5. Plane A covers three fourths of its route in the same time it takes plane D to cover one fourth of its route. At the exact moment that the two planes reach these positions, how many miles apart are they?

_____

6. You can see from the picture that plane D will eventually find the ship. How many miles must plane D travel before it is directly above the ship?

_____

Sugar Cube Puzzle

You will need a box of small cubes or sugar cubes
(the kind that really are shaped like a cube) for
this activity. Use 64 cubes to build one large cube.

How many small cubes will be on each edge of
the large cube? _____

Pretend that you are going to paint the entire
outside of the cube red (including the bottom).
When you are finished painting, how many small
cubes do you think will have:

Exactly 0 red faces? _____

Exactly 1 red face? _____

Exactly 2 red faces? _____

Exactly 3 red faces? _____

More than 3 red faces? _____

Now test your guess. "Paint" the cube with a red
(or any other color) marker. Separate the cubes
and compare the results with your estimate.

Try this activity one more time with clean sugar
cubes. Make a large cube that is either larger or
smaller than the first one you made.

What generalizations can you make about:

► The number of small cubes with more than 3 painted faces? _____

► The number of small cubes with exactly 3 painted faces?

_____

Describe how you could predict the number of cubes with:

► Exactly 2 painted faces _____

_____

► Exactly one painted face _____

_____

► Exactly zero painted faces _____

_____

Name _____

Area, Surface Area, and Volume

Dear Family,
 Our class is learning about area, surface area, and volume. Below are examples of the key math skills we have been studying.

Find the perimeter and the area of each figure.

1.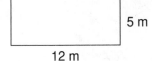

5 m

12 m

2.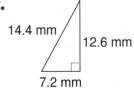

14.4 mm

12.6 mm

7.2 mm

3.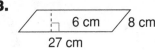

6 cm   8 cm

27 cm

_____   _____   _____

4. Study the circle below and find the area.

Use 3.14 for π. _____

r = 16 cm

Find the total surface area of each space figure.
Use 3.14 for π.

5.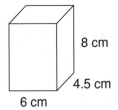

8 cm

4.5 cm

6 cm

6.   r = 5.3 cm

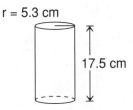

17.5 cm

_____   _____

Find the volume in cubic centimeters of each figure.

7.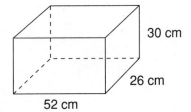

30 cm

26 cm

52 cm

8.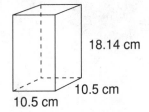

18.14 cm

10.5 cm

10.5 cm

_____   _____

Get the Point

Find the volume of the shaded section of each figure.
Use 3.14 for π.

1.

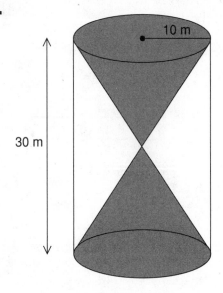

10 m

30 m

_____

2.

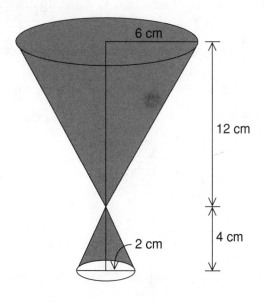

6 cm

12 cm

4 cm

2 cm

_____

3.

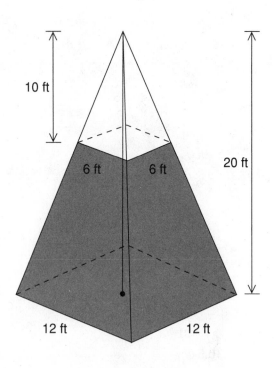

10 ft

6 ft   6 ft

20 ft

12 ft   12 ft

_____

4.

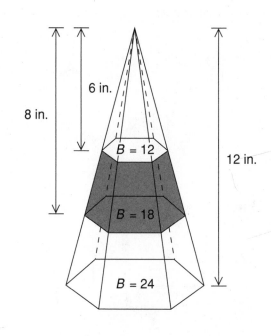

6 in.

8 in.

B = 12

B = 18

12 in.

B = 24

_____

Name _____

Planetary Facts

The nine planets vary in size from Pluto, the
smallest, to Jupiter, the largest. Jupiter is
approximately 45 times as large as Pluto.

Use your calculator to complete the table.
Use $\pi = 3.14$.

	Planet	Diameter at Equator	Radius	Circumference
1.	Mars	4,200 mi		
2.	Mercury		1,515 mi	
3.	Earth		3,963 mi	
4.	Pluto	1,900 mi		
5.	Venus	7,520 mi		
6.	Saturn		37,300 mi	
7.	Neptune	30,200 mi		
8.	Jupiter		44,350 mi	
9.	Uranus	31,570 mi		

Use the data in the table to solve these problems.

10. How much greater is the circumference
of Jupiter than the circumference of
Pluto?

_____

11. How much greater is the circumference
of Jupiter than the circumference of
Earth?

_____

12. What is the circumference of Earth in
feet?

_____

13. If an airplane circled the Earth one time
at an altitude of 6.6 miles, how far did
it travel?

_____

Weights And Logic

The Trenton Twins, Teri and Tina, are always fair. They make certain that their book bags weigh exactly the same when they walk home from school. They take the same courses, so they need only one copy of each book for homework.

Use the following facts to decide what each girl carries.

1. The math book plus the English book weigh the same as the science book.

2. The French book plus their gym clothes together weigh the same as the math book.

3. The math book and the history book weigh the same.

4. Teri insists upon carrying the heaviest textbook.

5. The two notebooks weigh the same.

6. The person who carries the gym clothes always carries the history book.

Teri carries:

_____

_____

_____

_____

Tina carries:

_____

_____

_____

_____

Tic-Tac-Toe

Select any equation from below and solve it. If the
answer is on the tic-tac-toe board, put an x on it. You
win when you get two tic-tac-toes, three in a row.

8	99	112
2	54	78
40	62	31

Solve these equations using mental math.

1. $t - 34 = 78$

_____

2. $x - 35 = 40$

_____

3. $y + 13 = 63$

_____

4. $k + 50 = 125$

_____

5. $25m = 200$

_____

6. $7h = 217$

_____

7. $\frac{8}{9}t = 64$

_____

8. $\frac{3}{4}n = 30$

_____

9. $76 = 12 + x$

_____

10. $34 = x - 20$

_____

11. $78 = \frac{2}{3}r$

_____

12. $270 = 5x$

_____

13. $\frac{1}{4}n = 6$

_____

14. $80x = 640$

_____

15. $p + 69 = 100$

_____

16. $\frac{2}{5}r = 16$

_____

17. $y - 48 = 64$

_____

18. $83 = 15 + t$

_____

Opening Factors

K. C. Locke, the prison warden, decided to free his prisoners
for good behavior. The cells were numbered from 1 to 25.
Each had a lock that opened when you turned it once and
locked when it was turned again, and so on.

Afraid that he might get in trouble if he let all the prisoners out
at once, he decided on a plan that would unlock some of the
cells, but not all. First he turned all the locks once, then he
went back and gave every second lock (2, 4, 6, 8, . . .) a turn.
Continuing, he gave every third lock a turn, every fourth a
turn, every fifth a turn, and so on all the way to every twenty-
fifth (of course, he turned only one lock for every thirteenth
and above).

How many prisoners did he set free?

_____

Use the table to keep track of each turn with a check mark
below the appropriate cell numbers.

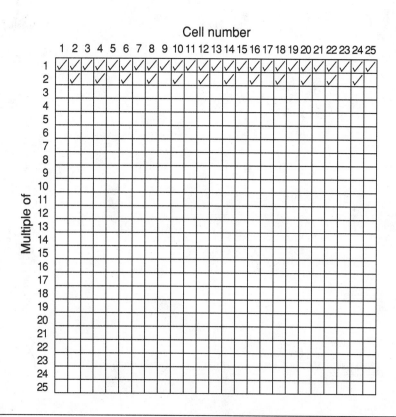

In-Verse Inverse

Give the inverse operation for each activity.

1. 1, 2, buckle my shoe. _____

2. 3, 4, close the door. _____

3. 5, 6, pick up sticks. _____

4. 7, 8, lay them straight. _____

5. 9, 10, begin again. _____

Show the inverse operation to get each variable
alone. Some may require two or more operations.

6. $\frac{x}{9}$ _____

7. $3a$ _____

8. $y - 17$ _____

9. $2p + 9$ _____

10. $\frac{y}{3} - 17$ _____

11. $34.2x + 8$ _____

12. $\frac{2b}{9}$ _____

13. $\frac{13a}{7} + 12$ _____

Start with the Solution

Write one addition equation and one subtraction equation for
the given solution.

1.

$n = 8$

_____

_____

2.

$y = 10$

_____

_____

Write one multiplication equation and one division equation
for the given solution.

3.

$x = 3$

_____

_____

4.

$r = 12$

_____

_____

Write a number in each box so that the given solution is correct.

5. $\boxed{}\, y = 32$

$y = 8$

6. $m - \boxed{} = 26$

$m = 43$

7. $\dfrac{p}{\boxed{}} = 12$

$p = 48$

8. $\boxed{}\, g = 20$

$g = 4$

9. $w - \boxed{} = 36$

$w = 47$

10. $\boxed{}\, f = 36$

$f = 2$

11. $\dfrac{\boxed{}}{k} = 4$

$k = 7$

12. $\dfrac{\boxed{}}{b} = 4$

$b = 20$

13. $\boxed{} + a = 36$

$a = 17$

Name _____

Checks and Balances

Many people write checks to pay their bills. When you write a check, you are telling the bank to pay someone with money from your account. Your bank will cash your check only if it is written correctly. Make this check out to your parents for $150.00 for rent.

After a check is written, it is important to keep record of the check number, the date, the person to whom the check was made, and the amount. Below is a typical check register used to record checks as they are written. The amount of each check is subtracted from the balance in order to know how much money is in the account at any time. Deposits are added to the balance.

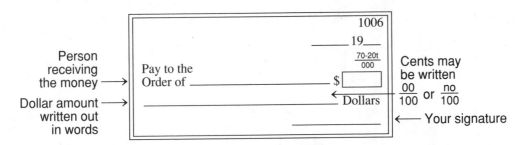

Record the check above in the register. Then record the following checks and deposit. Find the balance each time.

1. Check #1007
(Today's date)
Auto P. Car Insurance
$185.00

2. Check #1008
(Today's date)
Semi-Bright Electric Co.
$39.99

3. (Today's date)
Deposit
$450.00

4. Check #1009
(Today's date)
Jim's Hardbody Gym
$129.00

	Number	Date	Description of Transaction	Amount of Deposit	Amount of Payment or Withdrawal	Balance Forward
						$395.00
1.						
2.						
3.						
4.						

Using Critical Thinking

Use 100 tiles to make rectangles.
How many different rectangles can be arranged
with no more than 10 tiles on a side?

A 3 X 5 arrangement is the same

as a 5 X 3 arrangement.

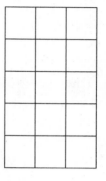
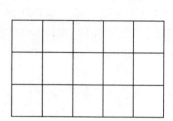

Complete the table by checking off all the possibilities.

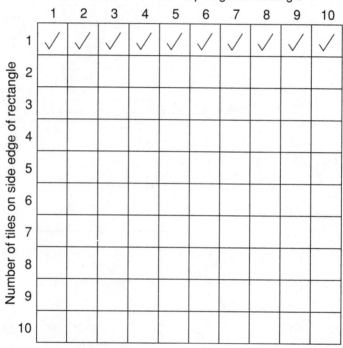

Number of tiles on top edge of rectangle

	1	2	3	4	5	6	7	8	9	10
1	✓	✓	✓	✓	✓	✓	✓	✓	✓	✓
2										
3										
4										
5										
6										
7										
8										
9										
10										

Number of tiles on side edge of rectangle

1. What is the total number of rectangles possible? _____

2. Write an equation for finding the number of possible rectangles.

_____

3. Using 144 tiles, how many rectangles can you arrange

with no more than 12 tiles on a side? _____

Sum It Up

The symbol Σ is a summation sign. It means "add a list of numbers."

$$\sum_{k=3}^{8} (K + 2)$$

This expression stands for the number 45: it is the sum of all the values for $(K + 2)$, from $K = 3$ to $K = 8$.

$$
\begin{aligned}
(3 + 2) &= 5 \\
(4 + 2) &= 6 \\
(5 + 2) &= 7 \\
(6 + 2) &= 8 \\
(7 + 2) &= 9 \\
(8 + 2) &= 10 \\
\hline
&\ 45
\end{aligned}
$$

You can evaluate this summation by finding all the $(K + 2)$ values and adding them together.

Evaluate each of the following.

1. $\displaystyle\sum_{x=-2}^{5} (x - 3)$ _____

2. $\displaystyle\sum_{l=1}^{6} 2l$ _____

3. $\displaystyle\sum_{t=-3}^{3} t^2$ _____

4. $\displaystyle\sum_{k=-2}^{2} (3k - 1)$ _____

5. $\displaystyle\sum_{n=-1}^{4} (n + 1)^2$ _____

6. $\displaystyle\sum_{x=0}^{5} 2^x$ _____

See if you can determine the summation expression for each sum. Then evaluate.

7. $2 + 4 + 6 + 8 + 10$

8. $6 + 7 + 8 + 9 + 10 + 11 + 12$

_____   _____

Solving Equations on the Calculator

Use the calculator codes to solve these two-step equations.

Equation	Code	Solution
1. $2x + 6 = 30$	30 $-$ 6 $=$ $\div$ 2 $=$	$x =$ _____
2. $5x - 15 = 35$	35 $+$ 15 $=$ $\div$ 5 $=$	$x =$ _____
3. $\frac{x}{15} + 7 = 10$	10 $-$ 7 $=$ $\times$ 15 $=$	$x =$ _____
4. $\frac{x}{5} - 12 = 3$	3 $+$ 12 $=$ $\times$ 5 $=$	$x =$ _____

To make your own calculator code, think about "undoing" the equation. Follow these steps:

► Enter the number to the right of the equal sign.
► Undo addition with subtraction.
► Undo subtraction with addition.
► Undo division with multiplication.
► Undo multiplication with division.
► Push $=$ for the solution.

Write the calculator code and find the solution for each equation.

	Code	Solution
5. $7x + 26 = 89$	_____	_____
6. $12x - 15 = 189$	_____	_____
7. $\frac{x}{4} + 36 = 46$	_____	_____
8. $\frac{x}{21} + 9 = 12$	_____	_____
9. $50x - 148 = 152$	_____	_____
10. $17x - 145 = 450$	_____	_____
11. $125x + 218 = 968$	_____	_____
12. $75x - 317 = 733$	_____	_____

What's Your Function

A function is a special relation that matches each
first member of a pair with only one second
member.

Examples of functions:

Bob's mother is Karen.   Bob has only one mother.

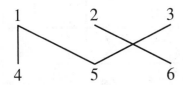

                                          Each first number is matched to only one
                                          second number.

Examples of relations that are not functions:

Karen's 2 sons are Bob and Eric.   Karen has 2 sons.

1 is matched with two second numbers.

Tell whether each of the following relations is a
function. For those not functions, give another
possible second number.

1. $x = 3$ **2.** $x \geq 7$

_____   _____

3. $x \angle 3$ **4.** $x + 5 = 9$

_____   _____

5. Roya is younger than Peter. _____

6. Cindy's cousin is Joel's.   _____

7. Bonnie's age is 15.   _____

Three Formulas

There are three formulas involving distance, rate, and time.

To find the distance use:	To find the rate use:	To find the time use:
$d = rt$	$r = \dfrac{d}{t}$	$t = \dfrac{d}{r}$

Use one of the formulas to solve each problem.

1. $r = 40$ km/h
   $t = 3$ h

   $d =$ _____km

2. $r = 55$ km/h
   $d = 385$ km

   $t =$ _____h

3. $t = 12$ s
   $d = 216$ m

   $r =$ _____m/s

Complete the table.

4.

r	35 m/s	28 m/h		145 km/h		130 cm/s
t	8s		6.5 h		15 h	3.5 s
d		252 m	780 km	725 km	6,780 km	

Solve.

5. A swimmer swam a distance of 2,000 m in 50 min. How many meters per minute was this?

6. A boat was rowed at a rate of 4.5 km/h across a lake 18 km wide. How long did it take to row across the lake?

_____   _____

Expression Patterns

In the table below, two expressions are evaluated
for several values of c. Notice that both expressions
are equal to 24 when $c = 8$.

c	1	2	3	4	5	6	7	⑧	9	10	11	12
$c + 16$	17	18	19	20	21	22	23	24	25	26	27	28
$32 - c$	31	30	29	28	27	26	25	24	23	22	21	20

Complete the table. Then ring the value of the variable
when the two expressions have the same value.

1.

n	1	2	3	4	5	6	7	8	9	10	11	12
$9 + n$												
$17 - n$												

2.

f	1	2	3	4	5	6	7	8	9	10	11	12
$30 - f$												
$12 + f$												

3.

t	1	2	3	4	5	6	7	8	9	10	11	12
$23 - t$												
$t + 9$												

4.

x	1	2	3	4	5	6	7	8	9	10	11	12
$x + 9$												
$31 - x$												

5. Write an addition and a subtraction
expression using the variable r. Make
both expressions have the same value
when $r = 3$.

6. Write an addition and a subtraction
expression using the variable y. Make
both expressions have the same value
when $y = 6$.

_____ _____   _____ _____

More Expression Patterns

The expressions $5n$, $n + 12$, and $\dfrac{45}{n}$ have the same values when $n = 3$.

n	1	2	③	4	5	6	7	8	9	10
$5n$	5	10	15	20	25	30	35	40	45	50
$n + 12$	13	14	15	16	17	18	19	20	21	22
$\dfrac{45}{n}$	45	22.5	15	11.25	9	7.5	6.43	5.625	5	4.5

Complete each table. Round decimals to the nearest hundredth.
Then ring the value of the variable when the two expressions
have the same value.

1.

h	1	2	3	4	5	6	7	8		10
$3h$										
$\dfrac{243}{h}$										

2.

c	1		3	4	5	6	7	8	9	10
$8c$										
$18 - c$										
$\dfrac{32}{c}$										

3.

y	1	2	3	4	5		7	8	9	10
$3y$										
$12 + y$										
$24 - y$										
$\dfrac{108}{y}$										

4. Write a multiplication and a division expression using the variable m. Make both expressions have the same value when $m = 2$.

_____ _____

5. Write a multiplication and a division expression using the variable t. Make both expressions have the same value when $t = 4$.

_____ _____

Name _____

Solving Equations

Dear Family,
    We studied equations and functions in algebra. We learned how to solve equations. Below are examples of the math skills we have been studying.

Write an expression for each phrase.

1. A number a increased by 33 _____

2. The difference when a number n is taken from 112 _____

3. The quotient when 19 is divided by t _____

4. b times 27 _____

Solve the equations.

5. $s + 29 = 100$ _____
6. $n + 5.5 = 8.7$ _____

7. $m - 35.4 = 26.57$ _____
8. $p - 329 = 264$ _____

9. $12t = 108$ _____
10. $6.5z = 53.95$ _____

11. $\frac{y}{9} = 20$ _____
12. $\frac{r}{5} = 8.4$ _____

13. $\frac{h}{2} - 2 = 1$ _____
14. $2w - 12 = 20$ _____

15. $15x + 14 = 59$ _____
16. $\frac{a}{2} + 1.2 = 8.2$ _____

Use the formula below to complete the table.

$W = \dfrac{4(h - 150)}{5} + 50$

W = weight in kilograms
h = height in centimeters

	Height	Weight
17.	175 cm	
18.	190 cm	
19.	160 cm	
20.	210 cm	

Zero Out

This game can be played with 2 or more players.

You will need one number cube and paper and pencil for each player.

Rules:

1. The first player rolls the number cube twice. The first roll gives the first number and the second roll determines the sign of that number. An odd number means a negative sign and an even number means a positive sign. Players record their numbers.

2. The players take turns rolling the number cube twice until each player has 3 signed numbers.

3. Each player then uses his or her signed numbers to try and make sums that zero out.

4. If a player can do so with her or his first 3 numbers, he or she wins. If not, play continues one double roll at a time until one player can zero out.

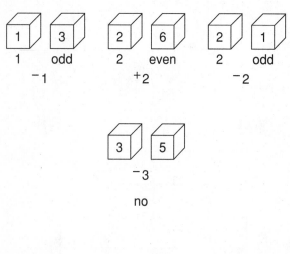

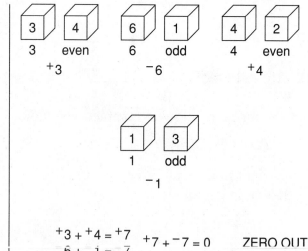

Name _____

Integer Puzzles

Use the given numbers to make each equation true.

3	5	7
⁻3	⁻5	⁻7

1. _____ + _____ = ⁻4 **2.** _____ + _____ = 8

3. _____ + _____ = 2 **4.** _____ + _____ = 4

5. _____ + _____ = ⁻12 **6.** _____ + _____ = ⁻2

7. _____ + _____ = 12 **8.** _____ + _____ = 10

9. _____ + _____ = 2 **10.** _____ + _____ = ⁻8

11. _____ + _____ = ⁻10 **12.** _____ + _____ = 0

2	6	9
⁻2	⁻6	⁻9

13. _____ + _____ = ⁻11 **14.** _____ + _____ = ⁻7

15. _____ + _____ = 4 **16.** _____ + _____ = ⁻4

17. _____ + _____ = 15 **18.** _____ + _____ = ⁻15

19. _____ + _____ = ⁻8 **20.** _____ + _____ = 7

21. _____ + _____ = 3 **22.** _____ + _____ = 11

23. _____ + _____ = 8 **24.** _____ + _____ = ⁻3

Make eight different addition equations using the given
numbers for the addends. Then
find each sum.

3	4	8
⁻3	⁻4	⁻8

25. ___ + ___ = ___ **26.** ___ + ___ = ___

27. ___ + ___ = ___ **28.** ___ + ___ = ___

29. ___ + ___ = ___ **30.** ___ + ___ = ___

31. ___ + ___ = ___ **32.** ___ + ___ = ___

Four in a Line

▶ Pick a number from Card A and subtract it from a number on Card B. Write your numbers and answer in the column on the right.

▶ Put an X on your answer on the game board.

▶ Pick two more numbers and try again. The object is to get four answers in a line on the game board. How many tries will it take?

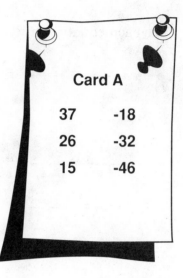

Card A

37	-18
26	-32
15	-46

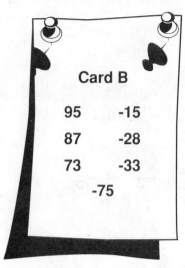

Card B

95	-15
87	-28
73	-33
	-75

	⁻59			⁻43	
	31	61	⁻70	80	
58	141	⁻65	105	17	47
⁻43	⁻10	⁻30	3	50	18
127	58	4	133	⁻52	72
113	⁻15	69	⁻54	91	58
	⁻41	⁻1	⁻48	13	
	⁻101	36	⁻90	⁻112	
	⁻43	⁻57	119	⁻29	

1. _____ − _____ = _____

2. _____ − _____ = _____

3. _____ − _____ = _____

4. _____ − _____ = _____

5. _____ − _____ = _____

6. _____ − _____ = _____

7. _____ − _____ = _____

8. _____ − _____ = _____

9. _____ − _____ = _____

10. _____ − _____ = _____

11. _____ − _____ = _____

12. _____ − _____ = _____

13. _____ − _____ = _____

14. _____ − _____ = _____

15. _____ − _____ = _____

Scores

Superior:	Good:	Need practice:
4 to 8 trials	9 to 14	15 or more

Number Puzzles

Work backward. Find each person's number.

1. Molly: If you multiply my number by ⁻4 and subtract 20, the result is 8. _____

2. Bruce: If you add 3 to my number, divide by 4 and then multiply by ⁻1, the result is ⁻2. _____

3. Walter: If you multiply my number by ⁻3, divide the result by 2 and add ⁻4, the result is 2. _____

4. Amy: If you divide my number by ⁻5 and subtract 2, the result is ⁻4. _____

5. John: If my number is multiplied by 2 and divided by 3, the result is the opposite of 4. _____

6. Leslie: If you multiply the opposite of my number by 6 and divide the result by 3 you get ⁻6. _____

7. Jason: If you double my number, add 2, divide by 20 and add ⁻1, the result is 0. _____

8. Barbara: If you multiply my number by ⁻3, subtract 4 and divide by ⁻5, the result is 5. _____

9. Susan: If you take the opposite of my number and multiply it by ⁻5, the result divided by ⁻8 is 5. _____

10. Wayne: My number multiplied by 6 and added to ⁻4 is equal to ⁻8 × 5. _____

Write some number problems of your own. Challenge classmates to find your number.

Magnifying the Problem

When you look at something through a magnifying lens, it usually has a bigger image. Some lenses also invert the image, that is, the lens turns the image upside down.

Suppose you have 4 different lenses.

A lens that magnifies twice is called 2.

A lens that magnifies three times is called 3.

A lens that magnifies twice and inverts is called ⁻2.

A lens that magnifies three times and inverts is called ⁻3.

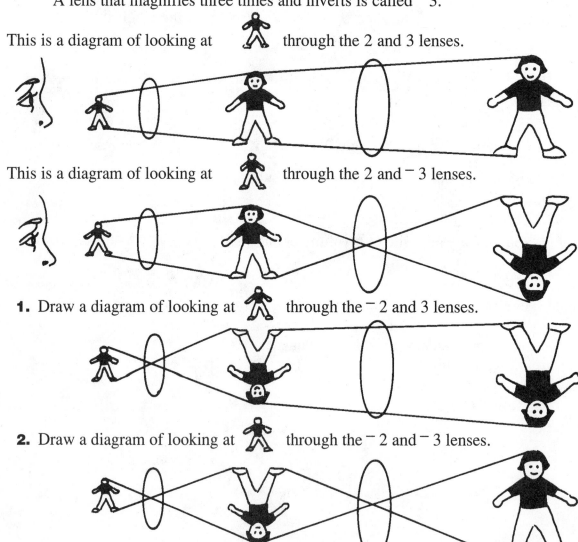

This is a diagram of looking at 👤 through the 2 and 3 lenses.

This is a diagram of looking at 👤 through the 2 and ⁻3 lenses.

1. Draw a diagram of looking at 👤 through the ⁻2 and 3 lenses.

2. Draw a diagram of looking at 👤 through the ⁻2 and ⁻3 lenses.

Secret Number Clues

Write and solve an equation for each secret number clue.

1.

> **Juan's Clue**
> If 8 is subtracted from my number the result is ⁻6.

_____

_____

2.

> **Carol's Clue**
> If you multiply my number by ⁻7 the product will be 56.

_____

_____

3.

> **Ginny's Clue**
> When 14 is added to my secret number the result is 5.

_____

_____

4.

> **Chuck's Clue**
> If you divide my number by ⁻12 the quotient is equal to ⁻5.

_____

_____

5.

> **Li's Clue**
> If the opposite of 16 is added to my number the sum will be ⁻5.

_____

_____

6.

> **Duane's Clue**
> I subtracted ⁻12 from my secret number and got an answer of 8.

_____

_____

Write your own secret number clues.
Then write and solve equations to find the secret numbers.

Lost but Not Forgotten

Be a mathematical private eye. Find each lost
number by writing an equation and then solving it.

1. Double the lost number is ⁻44.

    equation _____

    lost number _____

2. The sum of the lost number and 87 is
⁻98. _____

_____

3. 7 subtracted from the lost number is
15. _____

_____

4. The product of ⁻6 and the lost
number is 102. _____

_____

5. 10 more than the lost number is ⁻66.

_____

_____

6. 17 less than the lost number is ⁻80.

_____

_____

7. The lost number divided by ⁻9 is 54.

_____

_____

8. Triple the lost number is ⁻204.

_____

_____

9. ⁻29 subtracted from the lost number is
128. _____

_____

10. The product of the lost number and
⁻19 is ⁻152. _____

_____

11. The sum of the lost number and 43 is
⁻2. _____

_____

12. The lost number multiplied by ⁻4 is
344. _____

_____

13. 18 more than the lost number is ⁻123.

_____

_____

14. The lost number divided by 7 is ⁻581.

_____

_____

15. ⁻23 less than the lost number is 5.

_____

_____

16. The lost number multiplied by ⁻13 is
520. _____

_____

17. ⁻8 added to the lost number is 0.

_____

_____

18. 5 times the lost number is ⁻835.

_____

_____

Name _____

Using Integers

Compare the integers. Write $>$ or $<$ for each $\bigcirc$.

1. $^-8 \bigcirc {}^-12$ **2.** $^-10 \bigcirc {}^-4$ **3.** $19 \bigcirc {}^-19$

Add or subtract.

4. $2 + {}^-12$ _____   **5.** $^-8 - 5$ _____

6. $13 - 20$ _____   **7.** $^-4 + {}^-6$ _____

Multiply or divide.

8. $4 \times {}^-16$ _____   **9.** $^-9 \times {}^-20$ _____

10. $^-72 \div {}^-9$ _____   **11.** $^-105 \div 35$ _____

Solve the equations.

12. $h + 2 = {}^-12$ _____   **13.** $s - 15 = {}^-7$ _____

14. $\dfrac{x}{-2} = -19$ _____   **15.** $14b = {}^-28$ _____

Write and solve equations for problems 16 and 17.

16. Tom chose an integer and subtracted 9 from it. The difference was $^-7$. What was the integer?

_____

17. Rayette said, "I am thinking of an integer. If I multiply it by 4 and then add 7, the sum is $^-13$. What integer did Rayette think of?

_____

Answers: 1. $>$ **2.** $<$ **3.** $>$ **4.** $^-10$ **5.** $^-13$ **6.** $^-7$ **7.** $^-10$ **8.** $^-64$ **9.** 180 **10.** 8 **11.** $^-3$ **12.** $h = {}^-14$ **13.** $s = 8$ **14.** $x = 38$ **15.** $b = {}^-2$ **16.** $x - 9 = {}^-7; x = 2$ **17.** $4x + 7 = {}^-13; x = {}^-5$

Nutty Problems

Each nut bread contains walnuts, pecans, and Brazil nuts. How many of each type of nut does each nut bread contain?

1. This nut bread contains:
2 walnuts
Twice as many pecans as walnuts
10 nuts in all

_____

_____

2. This nut bread contains:
4 pecans
Half as many Brazil nuts as pecans
10 nuts in all

_____

_____

3. Walnuts make up half of this nut bread:
It has exactly 2 pecans
The number of walnuts is double the number of pecans

_____

_____

4. This nut bread contains:
The same number of pecans as walnuts
3 more Brazil nuts than pecans
A total of 18 nuts

_____

_____

5. This nut bread contains 12 nuts:
Half of the nuts are pecans
Walnuts make up $\frac{1}{4}$ of the nut bread

_____

_____

6. This nut bread contains at least 12 nuts:
It has one more walnut than pecans
It has one more pecan than Brazil nuts

_____

_____

7. This nut bread contains:
3 times as many pecans as Brazil nuts
One more walnut than Brazil nuts
6 nuts in all

_____

_____

8. This nut bread contains:
An equal number of pecans and Brazil nuts
5 more walnuts than pecans
No more than 20 nuts

_____

_____

Buried Treasure

Rosa is using a treasure map to find out how much money is really buried. All but one of the treasures are fake.

Start at (0,0). Follow the directions from each point. Describe your moves with positive and negative integers. Continue the pattern until you find the real treasure.

What is it? _____

A right 3, up 2   **B** right 4, up 1   **C** left 8, down 1   **D** left 6,   up 0   **E** right 2, up 8

_3_   _2_   _4_   _1_   _-8_   _-1_   ____ ____   ____ ____

F right 3, down 10 **G** right 0, down 7 **H** right 10, up 1   **I** right 3, up 5   **J** left 1, up 8

____ ____   ____ ____   ____ ____   ____ ____   ____ ____

K left 5,   up 1   **L** left 3,   down 3 **M** left 5,   up 4   **N** right 0, up 3

____ ____   ____ ____   ____ ____   ____ ____

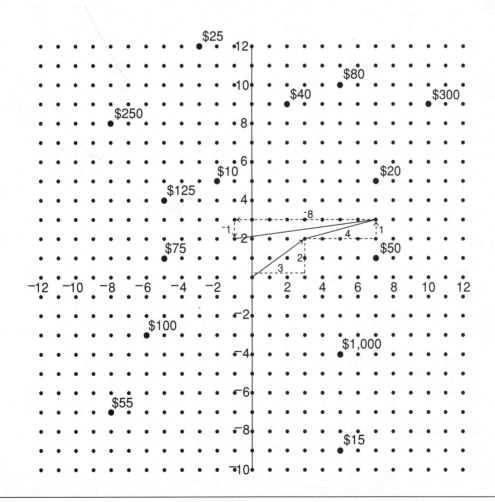

Temperature Charts

1. Marion noticed by watching television weather reports for one week that each day the temperature in Boston was exactly 6 degrees Celsius colder than in Washington D.C. She let x = Washington's temperature and y = Boston's temperature and wrote the equation:

$$y = x - 6.$$

Here are the temperatures she recorded from her window thermometer in Washington D.C., for the next week. What does she predict for the temperatures in Boston?

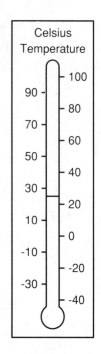

Celsius Temperature

	Sun.	Mon.	Tues.	Wed.	Thurs.	Fri.	Sat.
x	10	13	7	9	12	15	20
y							

2. Danny saw Marion's chart, but said that he could never distinguish cold temperatures from hot temperatures on a Celsius scale. He remembered a formula from science class:

$$F = \frac{9C}{5} + 32.$$

Complete the charts. Round answers to the nearest degree.

Washington Temperatures							
	Sun.	Mon.	Tues.	Wed.	Thurs.	Fri.	Sat.
C	10	13	7	9	12	15	20
F							

Boston Temperatures							
	Sun.	Mon.	Tues.	Wed.	Thurs.	Fri.	Sat.
C	4	7	1	3	6	9	14
F							

Name _____

Family Functions

1. No matter how old I get, my brother Peter is always 3 years older than I am. How old was Peter when I was 4?

_____

How old was Peter when I was born?

_____

Fill in the input-output table and graph the points on the grid.

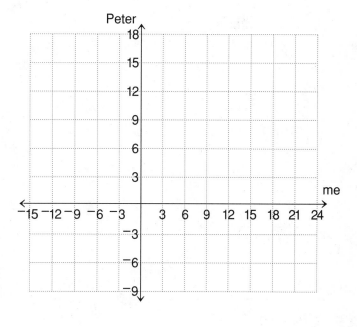

Me		2		6		13
Peter	3		7		12	

Do you need negative numbers on your graph? Explain.

_____

_____

2. Mrs. Marshall has two daughters, Beth and Lauren. She will not tell us their ages, but together their ages total 11 years.

How old is Beth if Lauren is 8? _____

How old is Lauren if Beth is 6? _____

Fill in the input-output table and graph the points on the grid.

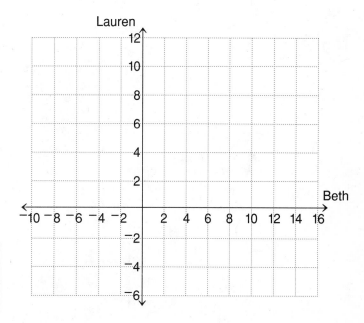

Beth	1		5	7		11
Lauren		3			9	

Write an equation that describes this situation. _____

Name _____

Picture This

Try these picture puzzles.
Pick the answer from the selection on the
right.

1.

A   B   C

2.

A   B

C   D

3.

A   B   C

Name _____

The Field of Factors

Can you help Patrick find his way home? To get
home, Patrick will walk across this field of tiles.
He may go up, down, right, or left (no diagonals),
but he may step only on tiles that are factors or
multiples of 36. Trace a path for Patrick.

To help you get started:

List all the factors of 36. _____

List the first 10 multiples of 36. _____

Start	108	8	342	56	11	104	101	7	41
5	9	55	12	360	252	2	3	57	126
49	36	15	324	30	150	25	4	21	19
81	216	1	144	126	200	56	180	55	300
41	104	10	101	57	288	18	72	324	8
19	200	49	25	5	6	15	10	81	30
300	7	150	11	21	18	36	216	2	Home

Divisibility in Social Studies

February 29 occurs only once every 4 years. We
call these leap years. A year that is divisible by 4
is a leap year.

Answer the following questions.

1. Is the present year a leap year? _____

2. Were you born in a leap year? _____

3. If you had been born on the February 29 that followed your birth, in what year would
you have been born? _____ How many birthdays would you have had by
now? (Remember: you would have a birthday only every 4 years. _____

The United States has a presidential election every
leap year. Were the following years election years
in the United States? If yes, do you know which
president won the election?

4. 1988 _____   **5.** 1956 _____

6. 1978 _____   **7.** 1936 _____

8. 1962 _____   **9.** 1960 _____

Some Basic Number Work

Type the following BASIC program into a computer.

Run it and see what happens.

```
10   PRINT "WHAT NUMBER DO YOU WISH
     TO CHECK?"

20   INPUT N

30   FOR X = 2 TO N/2

40   F = N/X

50   IF INT(F) = F THEN 90

60   NEXT X

70   PRINT N " IS PRIME."

80   GOTO 10

90   PRINT N " IS COMPOSITE."

100 GOTO 10
```

Can you explain how the program works?

Use the computer program to see if these numbers
are prime or composite.

1. 89   **2.** 103   **3.** 478

_____   _____   _____

4. 503   **5.** 1,009   **6.** 657

_____   _____   _____

7. 7,896   **8.** 1,993   **9.** 8,579

_____   _____   _____

Name _____

Calculator Patterns

Use your calculator to help find the patterns. If
your calculator shows error, complete the pattern
on your own.

1. $5 \times 11 + 5 = 60$ $5 \times$ _____

   $5 \times 111 + 5 = 560$ $5 \times$ _____

   $5 \times 1,111 + 5 =$ _____   _____

   $5 \times 11,111 + 5 =$ _____   _____

2. $5 \times 11 + 2 = 57$ _____

   $5 \times 111 + 3 =$ _____   _____

   $5 \times$ _____   _____

   $5 \times$ _____   _____

3. $6 \times 2 + 1 = 13$ _____

   $6 \times 22 + 2 = 134$ _____

   _____   _____

   _____   _____

4. $8 \times 1 + 1 = 9$ _____

   $8 \times 12 + 2 = 98$ _____

   $8 \times 123 +$ _____   _____

   _____   _____

   _____

Big Factor Trees

These factor trees are very large. Form groups of
3 or 4 students. Use calculators to help you divide
quickly, and see which student can correctly
complete these factor trees first. Check your work
by multiplying the final factors. Explain to other
members of your group what you did.

1. 7,200

2. 1,024

3. 60,750

4. 127,008

5. 1,000,000

6. 6,480

Problem Solving: Using the Strategies

1. Cory, Joe, Brenda, and Sandra were standing in line. Joe was not standing next to Cory or Brenda. Sandra was second in line. Cory was standing next to just one person. In what order were they standing?

_____

2. Two empty tanks of the same volume are being filled with water. Tank A starts filling 2 min before Tank B. Tank A fills at the rate of 60 min and Tank B at the rate of 75 min. How long after Tank B begins filling will the tanks contain the same amount of water?

_____

3. There were 20 people at a party. Each person shook hands with every other person. How many handshakes were there?

_____

4. An employer figured his total cost of hiring an employee. The employer multiplied the hourly wage he paid the employee by 1.3 and added $1. This gave the employer a rate of $14 per hour. How much was the employee paid per hour?

_____

5. Conway is 6 km east of Belltown. Lexington is 4 km east of Conway. Peach Valley is halfway between Belltown and Lexington. Where is Conway in relation to Peach Valley?

_____

6. Mrs. Clark is beginning an exercise program. She plans to walk 2 km for 2 days, 3 km for 3 days, 4 km for 4 days, and continue the pattern until she is walking 8 km per day. In how many days will she first walk 8 km?

_____

Greatest Common Factor

When it is difficult to find the greatest common
factor mentally, you can use the following method.

Example   Find the GCF of 105 and 396.

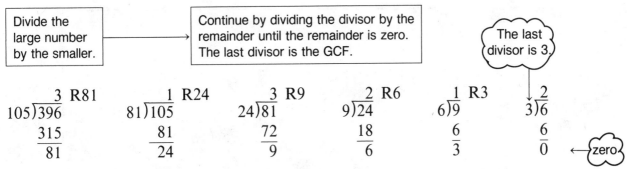

Since 3 is the last divisor, 3 is the GCF of 105 and 396.

Find the GCF of these numbers using the method above.

1. The GCF of 126 and 315 is _____.

2. The GCF of 93 and 217 is _____.

3. The GCF of 165 and 396 is _____.

4. The GCF of 504 and 567 is _____.

5. The GCF of 117 and 376 is _____.

6. The GCF of 119 and 375 is _____.

Seeing Stars

Connect pairs of points to show the lowest common multiple. If you do this correctly, you will see three shapes in your drawing. Shade them.

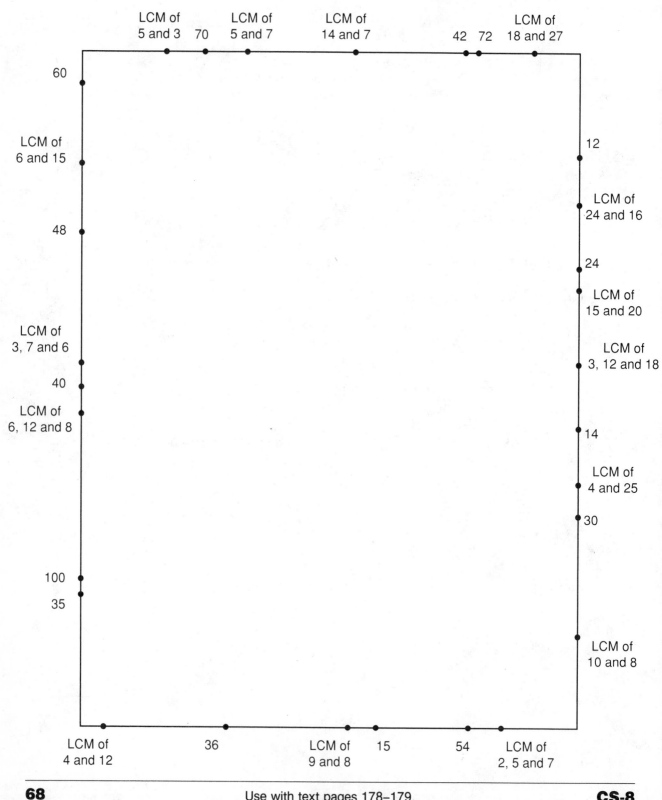

Name _____

Area and Population

The Five Largest States			The Five Smallest States		
State	Area (km²)	Population	State	Area (km²)	Population
Alaska	1,518,717	400,481	New Jersey	20,294	7,364,158
Texas	692,364	14,228,383	Hawaii	16,705	965,000
California	410,991	23,668,562	Connecticut	12,973	3,107,576
Montana	381,065	786,690	Delaware	5,327	595,225
New Mexico	315,096	1,299,968	Rhode Island	3,144	947,154

Use your calculator to solve the problems. Round
all answers that are not whole numbers to the
nearest hundredth.

1. How many times larger in area is Alaska than Texas? _____

2. Is the population of Texas more or less than the combined population
of New Jersey and Connecticut? How much more or less? _____

3. About how many Rhode Islands could be contained
inside Alaska? _____

4. Which state is most nearly 100 times the size of
Rhode Island in area? _____

5. True or false: The area of Alaska is large enough to contain the total
area of all the other states listed in the table except Montana. _____

6. The population density of a state is the number of people
living per square kilometer of area (Population ÷ Area).
What is the population density of Texas? _____

7. What is the population density of California? _____

8. Which state in the table has the smallest
population density? What is this density? _____

9. Which state in the table has the greatest population density?
What is this density? _____

Name _____

Unexpected Answers

Sometimes every bit of information in a
problem is very important. Can you solve these?

1. A woman is standing on a corner, wearing a mask.
Another woman runs up to her, and just before reaching
the masked woman, she turns and runs back in the
direction from which she came. What is happening?

_____

_____

_____

_____

2. Allen is sitting in his car. He starts it and drives west
in a straight line a quarter of a mile. When he stops
the car, he is facing east. How can this be?

_____

Try making up a riddle for your classmates.
Hint: Tell the facts but with an unusual point of view.

_____

_____

_____

_____

Name _____

Fraction Figures

Figure *ABCD* is 1 unit.

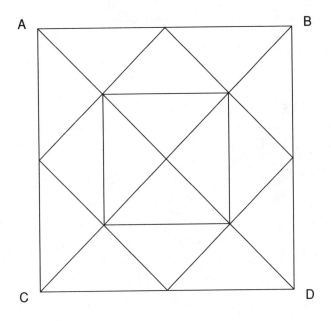

Write the fraction of figure *ABCD* each of these figures represents.

1. 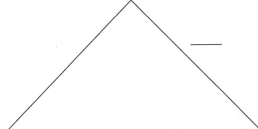 _____

2. 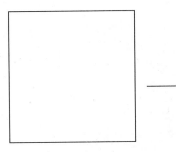 _____

3.  _____

4. 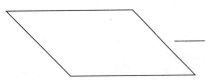 _____

5.  _____

6.  _____

Finding Pentagons

Find pairs of mixed numbers and improper fractions
that match. Draw straight lines to connect the pairs.
Use the dots to guide you. If you pair all the numbers
correctly, you should see two regular pentagons
formed by the lines. Shade them.

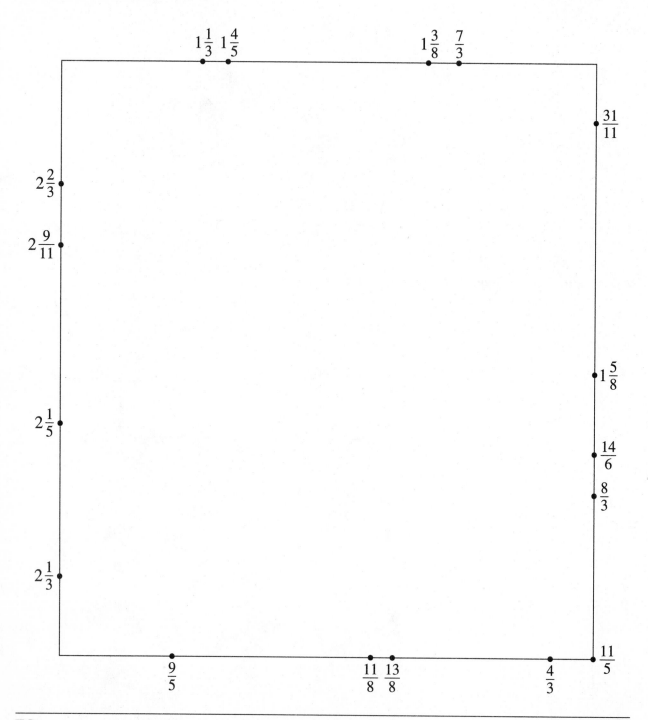

Making the Rounds

These numbers are the least and greatest numbers that
round to the same number. In the blank, write the number to
which they round.

1. 4.65

_____

4.74

2. 3.45

_____

3.54

3. 15.945

_____

15.954

4. 37.0165

_____

37.0174

These numbers are rounded to the nearest **tenth**. Write the
least and greatest numbers that would round to the given
number.

5. _____

0.8

_____

6. _____

0.1

_____

7. _____

13.2

_____

8. _____

5.0

_____

These numbers are rounded to the nearest **hundredth**.
Write the least and greatest numbers that would round to the
given number.

9. _____

6.17

_____

10. _____

0.34

_____

11. _____

17.06

_____

12. _____

23.09

_____

These numbers are rounded to the nearest **thousandth**.
Write the least and greatest numbers that would round
to the given number.

13. _____

45.018

_____

14. _____

9.001

_____

15. _____

0.035

_____

16. _____

0.176

_____

Five Alive

Dear Family,
   You can help your eighth grader recognize the many uses of fractions by pointing out their use in daily life. Some occasions for using fractions are measuring distances or objects, finding averages, designating time, and changing recipes.

Find pairs of equivalent fractions or decimals and connect them with straight lines. If you pair all the numbers correctly, you should see five triangles of equal size and similar shape formed by the lines.

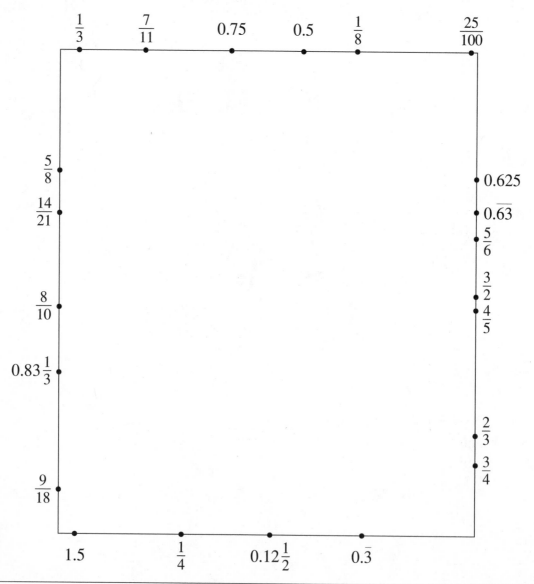

Star Trek

Find the answer for each problem. Then connect the dots for the answers in the same order as the problems. Getting all the answers correct can make you a star!

1. $\dfrac{-3}{10} + \dfrac{7}{10} =$ _____

2. $\dfrac{-5}{6} + \dfrac{-1}{6} =$ _____

3. $\dfrac{1}{2} + \dfrac{-4}{2} =$ _____

4. $\dfrac{1}{3} + \dfrac{-1}{2} =$ _____

5. $\dfrac{1}{4} - \dfrac{-1}{4} =$ _____

6. $\dfrac{1}{5} - \dfrac{4}{5} =$ _____

7. $\dfrac{2}{1} + \dfrac{-7}{3} =$ _____

8. $\dfrac{1}{4} - \dfrac{-3}{8} =$ _____

9. $\dfrac{7}{6} - \dfrac{-5}{6} =$ _____

10. $\dfrac{3}{4} + \dfrac{-5}{8} =$ _____

11. $\dfrac{9}{10} + \dfrac{-1}{2} =$ _____

• $\dfrac{1}{9}$ • $-\dfrac{1}{6}$ • 1 • $-2\dfrac{1}{4}$

-1 • $-\dfrac{3}{2}$ • $\dfrac{1}{2}$ • $-\dfrac{3}{5}$ • -4

• $\dfrac{1}{4}$ • $\dfrac{2}{3}$

• $\dfrac{2}{5}$ • $-\dfrac{1}{3}$

• $\dfrac{1}{10}$ • 2 • $-\dfrac{5}{6}$

• $\dfrac{3}{10}$ $\dfrac{1}{8}$ •   • $\dfrac{5}{8}$ • $\dfrac{7}{12}$

• $-\dfrac{4}{7}$

Name _____

Fraction Number-Line Subtraction

The diagram shows how to subtract fractions on a number line.

To find $3 - \frac{2}{3}$, go forward 3 units.

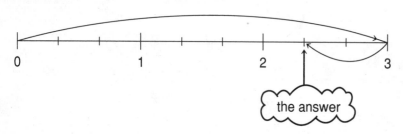

Then go backward $\frac{2}{3}$ unit.

the answer

Use the diagrams to complete these equations.
Write all fractions in lowest terms.

1. $4 - 1\frac{1}{2} = \boxed{}$

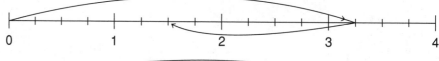

2. $3\frac{1}{4} - 1\frac{3}{4} = \boxed{}$

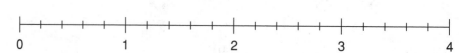

3. $3 - \boxed{} = \boxed{}$

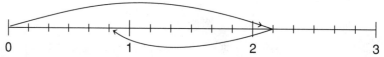

4. $1\frac{3}{5} - \boxed{} = \boxed{}$

5. $2\frac{1}{6} - \boxed{} = \boxed{}$

Draw a number line diagram to complete
each equation. Write all fractions in lowest terms.

6. $2\frac{1}{3} - 1\frac{2}{3} = \boxed{}$

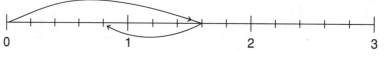

7. $3\frac{3}{5} - 2\frac{4}{5} = \boxed{}$

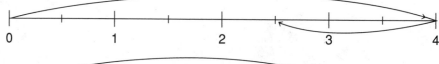

8. $3\frac{5}{8} - \frac{7}{8} = \boxed{}$

Use with text pages 202–203.

CS-8

Linking Expressions

Use the values in the box to help you link the
expressions and find the addends. Then use the
numbers in the sums to identify the coded words
at the bottom of the page. Evaluate the expressions
from left to right. Use a calculator to help you.

a	=	1
r	=	2
o	=	3
m	=	4
p	=	5
l	=	6
h	=	7
e	=	8
b	=	9
y	=	10

$4e - 14 \cdot r + 17 \cdot r \cdot y^2 \div y - 2h - (6 \cdot y^3) =$ ___ , ___ ___ ___

$85 \cdot 7r - y \div p + (4 \cdot 2y) \cdot r \cdot 3 =$ ___ , ___ ___ ___

$1 \cdot y \cdot p \cdot 3^2 - 6^2 - 2h \cdot o + (b \cdot p) =$ + ___ , ___ ___ ___
                                                                  _____

Sum A =   ___ , ___ ___ ___

$(y^6 \cdot r) + (y^5 \cdot p) + e^5 + 5^6 + (y^3 \cdot 20) -$
$(y^2 \cdot 2) - 7b + 3r =$ ___ , ___ ___ ___ , ___ ___ ___

$y^3 \cdot 25 + y^3 - m^4 + (3h + 10^2) + 10^6 +$
$(7 \cdot 10^5) =$ ___ , ___ ___ ___ , ___ ___ ___

$9 \cdot 10^5 + (10^3 \cdot 5b) + (7 \cdot 10^2) -$
$(5y + p) + 5b - h =$ + ___ ___ ___ , ___ ___ ___
                        _____

Sum B =   ___ , ___ ___ ___ , ___ ___ ___

Sum A   Sum B

___ ___ ___ ___   **I   S   N   O**   ___ ___ ___ ___
        1   **2** ___ **6** ___
___ ___ ___ ___   ___ ___ ___ ___

Triangle Tangle

Triangle *XYZ* represents one unit.

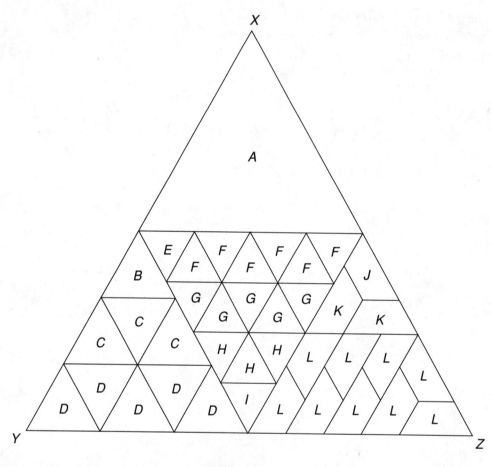

Complete each equation to show what fractional part of the whole triangle is represented by each letter.

$\frac{1}{4}$ of $1 = \frac{1}{4}$

1. *A* = _____

2. *B* = _____

3. Total of *C* = _____

4. Total of *D* = _____

5. *E* = _____

6. Total of *F* = _____

7. Total of *G* = _____

8. Total of *H* = _____

9. *I* = _____

10. *J* = _____

11. Total of *K* = _____

12. Total of *L* = _____

Fraction Equation Squares

Write a fraction or mixed number in each blank
square so that the equations across and down are
correct. Study the example

Example:

$1\frac{1}{4}$	•	$1\frac{1}{2}$	=	
•		•		•
$\frac{3}{4}$	•	$2\frac{1}{4}$	=	
=		=		=
	•		=	

$1\frac{1}{4} \cdot \frac{3}{4} \rightarrow$

$1\frac{1}{4}$	•	$1\frac{1}{2}$	=	$\frac{15}{8}$
•		•		•
$\frac{3}{4}$	•	$2\frac{1}{4}$	=	$\frac{27}{16}$
=		=		=
$\frac{15}{16}$	•	$\frac{27}{8}$	=	$\frac{405}{128}$

$1\frac{1}{4} \cdot 1\frac{1}{2}$

Use this square as a check.

1.

$3\frac{1}{8}$	•	$\frac{1}{4}$	=
•		•	•
$\frac{3}{8}$	•	$2\frac{3}{4}$	=
=		=	=
	•		=

2.

$2\frac{1}{3}$	•	$1\frac{5}{6}$	=
•		•	•
3	•		=	$\frac{2}{3}$
=		=	=
	•		=

3.

$2\frac{1}{8}$	•		=	$1\frac{3}{4}$
•		•	•
$3\frac{1}{4}$	•	$\frac{1}{2}$	=
=		=	=
	•		=

4.

$3\frac{1}{4}$	•		=	$2\frac{1}{2}$
•		•	•
	•		=
=		=	=
$\frac{3}{4}$	•		=	$1\frac{1}{2}$

Make a square of your own.

5.

$2\frac{5}{6}$	•		=	$4\frac{2}{3}$
•		•	•
	•		=
=		=	=
$1\frac{1}{2}$	•		=	2

6.

	•		=
•		•	•
	•		=
=		=	=
	•		=

Egyptian Division

Here are some Egyptian fraction symbols.

$$\rule{0pt}{0pt} = \frac{1}{2} \qquad \rule{0pt}{0pt} = \frac{1}{3} \qquad \rule{0pt}{0pt} = \frac{1}{4} \qquad \rule{0pt}{0pt} = \frac{1}{6} \qquad \rule{0pt}{0pt} = \frac{2}{3}$$

Use the symbols to make each equation true.

1. ☐ ÷ ☐ = _____

2. ☐ ÷ ☐ = _____

3. ☐ ÷ ☐ = _____

4. ☐ ÷ ☐ = _____

5. _____ ÷ ☐ = 2

6. _____ ÷ ☐ = 2

7. ☐ ÷ _____ = 4

8. ☐ ÷ _____ = $\frac{3}{8}$

9. _____ ÷ ☐ = ☐

10. ☐ ÷ _____ = ☐

11. _____ ÷ ☐ = ☐

12. 2 ÷ _____ = 3

Networks

The figures below are **networks**. A network is
traceable if you can start at one point and trace
the entire figure without lifting your pencil or
retracing any lines.

1. Which of these networks are traceable? _____

A
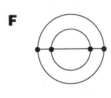
B

C
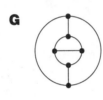
D
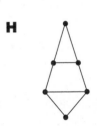

E

F

G

H

Vertices are the points where the lines meet. A vertex is odd if an
odd number of lines meet at that vertex. Otherwise, the vertex is
even.

2. Copy and complete this table for the networks above as well as
for ten more networks that you draw. Record the number of
odd vertices and the number of even vertices and whether each
network is traceable.

Network	Number of Odd Vertices	Number of Even Vertices	Traceable?
A	2	2	Yes
B			
C			

3. Can you find a pattern between the odd vertices and whether
the network is traceable?

_____

Elevens

This triangle of numbers
is Pascal's triangle.

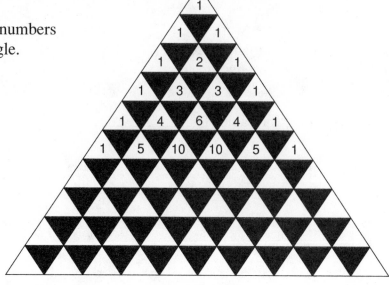

The pattern does not stop here. It continues.

1. Find the pattern of numbers and complete
the next 4 rows of the triangle.

The numbers in each row of the triangle
can be used to determine powers of 11.

$$1 = 11^0$$
$$11 = 11^1$$
$$121 = 11^2$$
$$1,331 = 11^3$$
$$14,641 = 11^4$$

The next row has 2-digit numbers.

$$1 \quad 5 \quad 10 \quad 10 \quad 5 \quad 1$$

Scientific notation can help you find
the value of 11^5.

$$(1 \times 10^5) + (5 \times 10^4) + (10 \times 10^3) + (10 \times 10^2)$$
$$+ (5 \times 10^1) + (1 \times 10^0)$$

$$100,000 + 50,000 + 10,000 + 1,000 + 50 + 1$$

$$161,051 = 11^5$$

2. Use scientific notation to expand the
9th row and find the value of 11^8. Do
the same for the 10th row.

It's All Relative

Tell which strategy you will use.
Solve.

1. Tom is 3 times as old as his sister. In 2 years he will be only twice as old as she is. How old is Tom now?

_____

_____

_____

_____

2. Toni can visit her uncle in the hospital on Monday, Wednesday or Friday at 1 p.m., 2 p.m., 3 p.m. or 4 p.m. How many choices for a visit does she have?

_____

_____

3. Toby wants to watch a television special at 10 p.m. Before watching it he needs to do 2 h of homework, make a 15 min phone call, and eat dinner and clean up which takes 1 h 15 min. At what time should he come home?

_____

_____

4. Tomas has 3 aunts and 2 uncles. Each aunt has 2 children and each uncle has 1 child. How many cousins does Tomas have?

_____

_____

5. Tina is $\frac{1}{4}$ as old as her father. In 5 years she will be $\frac{1}{3}$ as old as he is. How old will Tina be in 5 years?

_____

_____

6. Ted wants to play soccer, tennis or jog. He can join any one of 5 teams for each sport. How many choices does Ted have?

_____

_____

What problems are related? _____

Track Record

The first table below shows the Superior
Junior High track team's record of
competition against other schools.
Use the data to complete the second table.

High jump	100-m dash	400-m relay
9 wins	5 wins	7 wins
4 losses	5 losses	2 losses
1 tie	0 ties	1 tie

		Ratio
1.	High jump wins to high jump losses	
2.	100-m dash wins to number of dashes run	
3.	High jump wins to 400-m relay wins	
4.	100-m dash losses to 100-m dashes run	
5.	Total wins to total losses	
6.	400-m relay wins and ties to 400-m losses	
7.	High jump losses to high jump wins	
8.	100-m dash wins and ties to 100-m dashes run	
9.	100	5 to 5
10.		10 to 4
11.	400	7 to 10
12.		5 to 7
13.		8 to 10
14.		11 to 21
15.		7 to 21

Rates and Distances

Jesse and Bart begin walking in opposite directions
from the same point. Jesse walks 3 km each $\frac{1}{2}$ hr and
Bart walks 2.5 km each $\frac{1}{2}$ hr. Complete this table and
use it to solve Problems 1 and 2.

	Time	$\frac{1}{2}$ hr	1 hr	$1\frac{1}{2}$ hr	2 hr	$2\frac{1}{2}$ hr	3 hr	6 hr	8 hr
Distance walked (kilometers)	Jesse	3	6						
	Bart	2.5		7.5					
	Distance apart (km)	5.5							

1. How far apart are Jesse and Bart

after 1 hr? _____ after 2 hr?

_____ after $2\frac{1}{2}$ hr? _____

2. In how many hours are Jesse and Bart

11 km apart? _____ 33 km apart?

_____ 16.5 km apart? _____

Two dune buggies leave the same point at the same
time heading in opposite directions. The red one
travels 16 km/hr and the bronze one travels 10 km/hr.
Complete this table and solve the problems.

	Time	1 hr	2 hr	3 hr	4 hr	5 hr	6 hr	8 hr
Distance traveled (kilometers)	Red dune buggy							
	Bronze dune buggy							
	Distance apart (km)							

3. How far apart are the dune buggies

after 1 hr? _____ after 3 hr?

_____ after 5 hr? _____

4. In how many hours will the dune

buggies be 52 km apart? _____

26 km apart? _____

78 km apart? _____

Use with text pages 228–229.

The Division Game

Dear Family,

Here is a game designed to help students learn to use division to determine the unit price of an item. This skill will help students compare prices in stores. Along with the game board below, you will need 4 sets of number cards labeled 2 to 9 and a marker for each player.

Number of players: 2

Each player begins with his or her marker on the first money amount, $0.48.

The first player picks a card from the top of the shuffled deck. The player then divides $0.48 by the number picked. If there is a remainder, the player moves his or her marker a number of spaces equal to the remainder. If there is no remainder, the player may move the number of spaces equal to the number shown on the card. In either case, the space on which the player lands is divided to begin the next turn.

The second player plays in a similar way.

The first player to reach the finish line is the winner.

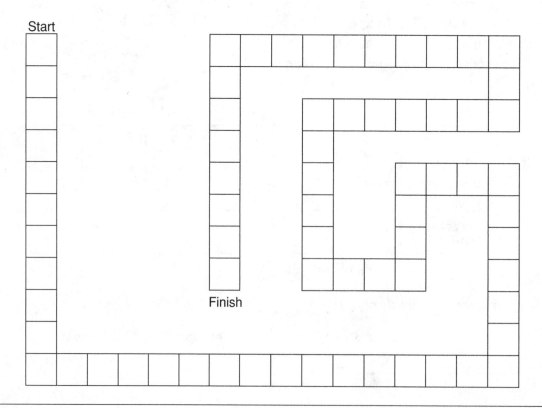

Start

Finish

Rectangle Ratios

Measure the lengh (*l*) and width (*w*) of each
rectangle with a centimeter ruler.

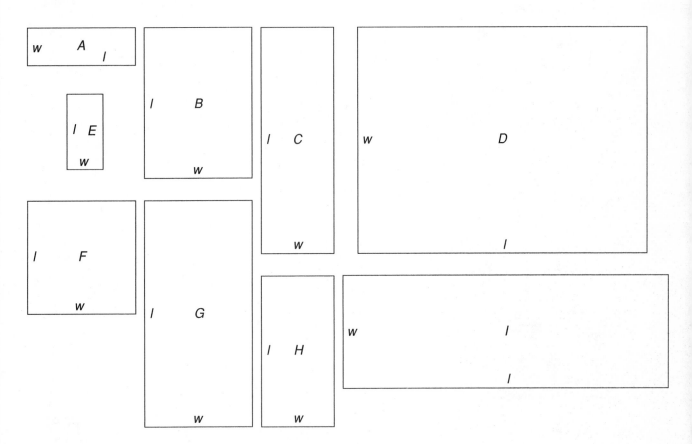

1. Write the width-length ratio for each rectangle.
Rectangle   *A*   *B*   *C*   *D*   *E*   *F*   *G*   *H*   *I*

2. Solve these proportions. In the blank below each
proportion, write the letters of the rectangles that
have the corresponding width-length ratios.

$$\frac{1}{3} = \frac{3}{\Box} \qquad \frac{3}{4} = \frac{\Box}{8} \qquad \frac{3}{9} = \frac{\Box}{6} \qquad \frac{2}{4} = \frac{3}{\Box} \qquad \frac{3}{6} = \frac{\Box}{2}$$

_____   _____   _____   _____   _____

Name _____

Enlarge the Pictures

Estimate the scale used to draw each of these pairs
of pictures. Then measure with a ruler to test your
estimate.

1.

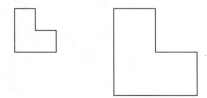

Estimate: _____

Scale: _____

2.

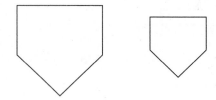

Estimate: _____

Scale: _____

3.

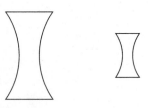

Estimate: _____

Scale: _____

4.

Estimate: _____

Scale: _____

Trace these pictures onto centimeter graph paper.
Mark enough points onto the grid to sketch an
enlargement in the given scale.

5.

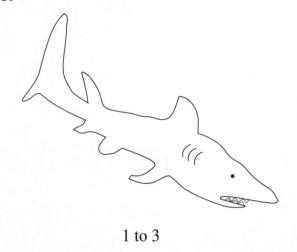

1 to 3

6.

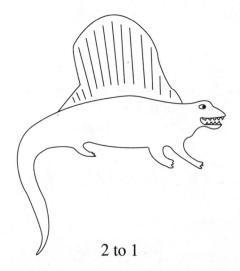

2 to 1

Use with text pages 234–235.

Golden Ratio Constructions

The Golden Ratio has been known since the time of
the ancient Greeks. It remains interesting today
because it is still used in architecture, art and design,
music, even in the study of human anatomy.

Here are two activities based on the Golden Ratio.

1. Any line segment can be separated into two
sections to demonstrate the Golden Ratio.

Place point Y on segment XZ so that the ratio of
XZ to YZ is as close to the Golden Ratio as you
can make it.

X Z

Complete each statement:

A Segment XZ = _____ cm

B Segment XZ = _____ cm

C Segment YZ = _____ cm

Complete the proportion:

$$\frac{xz}{yz} = \frac{12}{7.5} = \text{_____}$$

2. A Golden Rectangle can be split into
several smaller Golden Rectangles and
squares.

► Split the rectangle into a square and
a rectangle with a vertical line.

► What are the dimensions of the new
rectangle? Is it Golden?

_____

► What kind of line will split the new
rectangle into a square and a rectangle?

_____   5 cm

► Draw the line. What are the dimensions
of the new rectangle? What is the ratio of
its sides? Is it a Golden Rectangle?

_____

► If you continue the process will you
create any more Golden Rectangles?

Try it and see. _____

8 cm

Gaining Perspective

Have you ever wondered how a 2-dimensional painting creates the feeling that it has depth? Artists achieve this by using a concept related to mathematics: perspective. You can use this same concept to create similar figures.

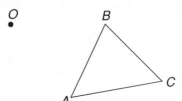

1. Trace the picture at the right onto a sheet of unlined paper.

2. Draw line segment $\overline{OA'}$, which passes through A and is exactly twice as long as OA.

3. Do the same with segments $\overline{OB'}$ and $\overline{OC'}$.

4. Draw triangle $A'B'C'$.

5. Measure each of these line segments to the nearest mm:

   AB = _____ mm AC = _____ mm BC = _____ mm

   $A'B'$ = _____ mm $A'C'$ = _____ mm $B'C'$ = _____ mm

6. Complete these ratios:

   $$\frac{AB}{A'B'} = \text{_____}$$ $$\frac{AC}{A'C'} = \text{_____}$$ $$\frac{BC}{B'C'} = \text{_____}$$

Do the triangles look similar? How could you check to see that they are similar?

_____

Triangles ABC and $A'B'C'$ are similar and are in the ratio 1 to 2. Use the same procedure to draw similar triangles that are in the scale of 1 to 3.

Do you get the feeling of 3-dimensional perspective from these pictures?

Problems, Problems, Problems

Problems like the ones you solved on page 240 of your text can be written by following a model. You can create problems like them yourself by using the series of steps below.

For example, follow the structure of this problem:

> Steven, Tom, Valerie, and Walt like to ski, bowl,
> __1__
> read, and swim. Valerie's hobby does not require
> __2__
> any special equipment. Tom and Walt like to stay
> __3__   __4__
> indoors for their hobbies. Walt's average has
>
> improved lately.

Number 1 gives the subject of the problem:
4 hobbies.

Number 2 separates Valerie's hobby from the other three hobbies.

Number 3 separates Tom's and Walt's hobbies from Steven's.

Number 4 separates Walt from Tom.

Now, solve this problem. What hobby does each have?

_____

_____

Next, change the subject of this problem from hobbies to something else. You might use foods that are enjoyed, after-school clubs, or places to visit. Use steps 2, 3, and 4 as they are used above to create your own problem. The structure will be the same, but the look will be completely different.

Another Ratio

The cosine ratio for acute angles of right triangles is:

$$\cos A = \frac{\text{length of adjacent side}}{\text{length of hypotenuse}}$$

$$\cos A = \frac{b}{c}$$

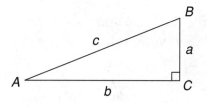

You can use this table of cosines to find the length x to the nearest tenth of a meter in each exercise.

Example:

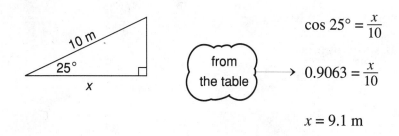

$$\cos 25° = \frac{x}{10}$$

from the table → $0.9063 = \frac{x}{10}$

$$x = 9.1 \text{ m}$$

Angle	Cos
20°	0.9397
25°	0.9063
30°	0.8660
35°	0.8192
40°	0.7660
45°	0.7071
50°	0.6428
55°	0.5736
60°	0.5000
65°	0.4226

1.

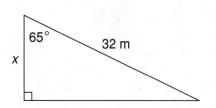

_____

2.

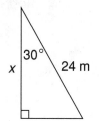

_____

3.

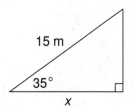

_____

4.

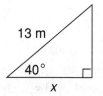

_____

Indirect Measurement

You have used a protractor to measure angles on paper. You can also use a protractor to measure lengths that cannot be easily reached. Examples are the height of a tree or even how high your kite is flying. You will need to make an instrument like a transit, a tool surveyors have been using for hundreds of years.

Here is what you will need: a protractor with a hole at the vertex, a drinking straw, and a paper clip.

Open the clip. Push it through the straw and the hole in the protractor.

The straw should rotate around the clip while sliding against the protractor.

To operate your transit, look past the clip through the straw.

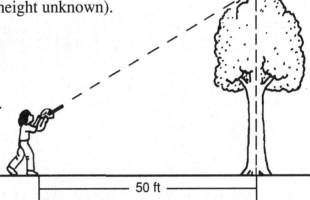

To test your transit, you will need: one tree (height unknown).

Follow these steps:

1. Estimate the height of the tree.

2. Pace off 50 feet from the base of the tree.

3. Hold the protractor level to the ground. Look through the straw until you see the top of the tree.

4. Note the angle that the straw makes with the bottom of the protractor

5. Use the tangent ratio to solve for the height of the tree.

How good was your estimate?

Several factors in this experiment will cause your result to be

a rough estimate. Which ones can you identify? _____

_____

_____

Use the instrument to measure other heights indirectly.

Calculator Curiosities II

Use your calculator to solve.

1. What is the largest number of Mondays that there can possibly be in one year?

_____

2. Some stores date their receipts this way:
  January 1 is 1
  January 2 is 2
  February 1 is 32
and so on. What number would be on the receipt when the year is exactly 40% over? What would the date be (if it were not a leap year)?

_____

3. The world indoor record for continuous seesawing is 1,101 h. If the seesawing began March 28, 1977, on what date did it end?

_____

4. If the record in Problem 3 began on a Wednesday, on what day of the week did it end?

_____

5. Stella was born in 1977. Her sister is 8 years younger than Stella. In what year will Stella be exactly 3 times as old as her sister?

_____

6. Draw a square around 3 rows of 3 dates in any month on a calendar. Is it a magic square? What patterns do you see in the square?

_____

_____

_____

Alphabet Percent Soup

Do you know that this sentence, "The quick brown
fox jumps over the lazy dog," contains all twenty-six
letters of the alphabet?

The message above has exactly 100 letters.

What percent of the message is each letter of the
alphabet?

Complete the table. Then complete Problems 1-4
below.

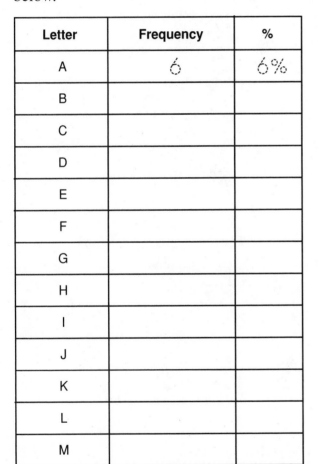

Letter	Frequency	%
A	6	6%
B		
C		
D		
E		
F		
G		
H		
I		
J		
K		
L		
M		

Letter	Frequency	%
N		
O		
P		
Q		
R		
S		
T		
U		
V		
W		
X		
Y		
Z		

1. What letter was the greatest percent of the message? _____

2. List the four letters that were the greatest percent of the message. _____

3. Which letters occurred in no more than 1% of the message? _____

4. Which letters occurred in 6% of the message? _____

Name _____

Area Hysteria

You can find the area of any geoboard figure by enclosing it in a rectangle and then subtracting the areas of the extra sections.

For example, to find the
area of this figure: Do this:

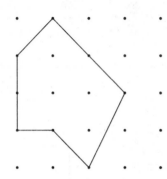

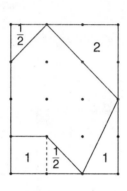

Area of the figure =
area of rectangle –
area of extra sections.

Area = $12 - (\frac{1}{2} + 2 + 1 + \frac{1}{2} + 1) = 7$ square units

1. Copy this figure. Find its area.
   Shade 37.5 percent of the figure.

_____

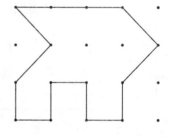

2. Copy this figure. Find its area.
   Shade $\frac{1}{9}$ of the figure.

_____

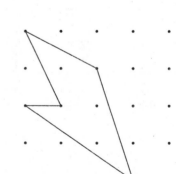

3. Draw geoboard figures so that you can
   exactly shade each of the following
   amounts. Then shade the given amount.
   A 20 percent   **B** one tenth   **C** 75 percent
   D one third   **E** 87.5 percent   **F** five sixths

Name _____

Geography Challenge

Below are outline maps of 5 of the 7 largest
countries in the world: Australia, Brazil, China,
India, and the United States. Can you identify
them? If not, use an atlas to help. Then write each
country's name inside the outline. Then answer
the questions below, rounding to the nearest whole
number when necessary. Use a calculator for the
computation.

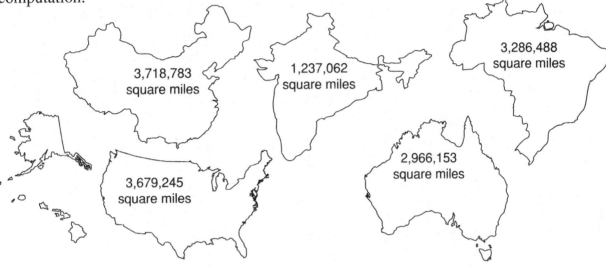

3,718,783
square miles

1,237,062
square miles

3,286,488
square miles

3,679,245
square miles

2,966,153
square miles

1. Rank the countries by name in order of size from largest to smallest. _____

_____

2. What percent of the area of the United States is the area of Brazil? _____

3. What percent of the area of China is the area of Australia? _____

4. What percent of the area of India is the area of Brazil? _____

5. What country has an area equal to 90 percent of the area of Brazil? _____

6. What country has an area equal to 112 percent of the area of Brazil? _____

7. The Soviet Union (U.S.S.R.), the largest country in the world, has an area of 8,600,387
   square miles. What percent of the Soviet Union's area is the combined area of the

   United States and China? _____

Name _____

On the Table

Use the multiplication table to answer the
questions below. First estimate, then determine
the exact percent.

×	1	2	3	4	5	6	7	8	9	10
1	1	2	3	4	5	6	7	8	9	10
2	2	4	6	8	10	12	14	16	18	20
3	3	6	9	12	15	18	21	24	27	30
4	4	8	12	16	20	24	28	32	36	40
5	5	10	15	20	25	30	35	40	45	50
6	6	12	18	24	30	36	42	48	54	60
7	7	14	21	28	35	42	49	56	63	70
8	8	16	24	32	40	48	56	64	72	80
9	9	18	27	36	45	54	63	72	81	90
10	10	20	30	40	50	60	70	80	90	100

What percent of the numbers below and to the
right of the double lines:

		Estimate	Actual
1.	Have only one digit?	_____	_____
2.	Have two digits?	_____	_____
3.	Contain a zero?	_____	_____
4.	Are prime numbers?	_____	_____
5.	Are perfect squares?	_____	_____
6.	Are multiples of 3?	_____	_____
7.	Are divisible by 5?	_____	_____
8.	Contain the digit 7?	_____	_____

Numbers, Numbers, Numbers

What is the product of this multiplication?

$$5,363,222,357$$
$$\times\ 2,071,723$$

If you have nothing to do for a while, you could multiply to find the product. However, here is a more interesting way.

Take the first 20% of the digits 1139176115. _____

Take the last 50% of 919111. _____

Take the first 37.5% of 11124184. _____

Take the second 20% of 3711815617. _____

Take the last 83.3% of 411111. _____

Take the first 25% of 11471006. _____

Now write all your answers in a row, insert commas where needed, and write the product:

_____

Name _____

Love Those Rebates

Dear Family,
    We are studying percent in class. Rebates are one application of percent. This game reinforces the idea that rebates and the concept of percent are related.

Appliances		
①	Hairdryer	$20
②	Microwave Oven	$120
③	Blender	$40
④	Portable Stereo	$60
⑤	Portable TV	$100
⑥	Telephone	$50

Rebates			
①	10%	②	20%
③	30%	④	40%
⑤	50%	⑥	60%

Number of players: 2 or 3

Equipment needed: 2 number cubes of different colors

How to play: Assign one number cube for appliances and one for rebates. The first player rolls both number cubes and calculates the amount of money saved on the purchase.

For example, if a player rolls 2 and 3, he or she purchases a microwave oven (2) for $120 with a 30% rebate (3). The player gets $36 back.

The player with the largest rebate total after five rounds is the winner.

Name _____

Win at Nim

Dear Family,
    Nim, a strategy game, is easy to learn to play, but more difficult to learn to win. There are many variations. Here are several. Each game is played with two players.

You will need 15 markers (coins or beans).

How to Play: Take turns. You may remove 1, or 2, or 3 markers. The person who removes the last marker loses.

What strategies can you use to make sure you do not pick up the last marker?

_____

_____

_____

Variations:

1. Arrange the markers in 3 rows as shown. Take turns. You may remove as few as 1 marker or as many as an entire row. You may not begin to remove markers from a row until the previous row has been completely removed. Again, if you must remove the last marker, you lose.

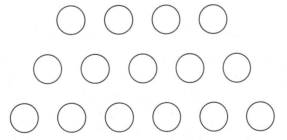

2. Reverse the rules. The object now is to remove the last marker. Do you see that different strategies are needed?

The Wise Shopper

How careful a shopper are you? Here is a chance to
find out.Get a supermarket flier or use a full-page
advertisement from your local newspaper. Copy
the chart below. You have $75 to spend. How close
can you come to spending all of it? Remember, you
cannot go over the $75. If several of your
classmates can get the same ad or flier, have a
contest to see who is the "best" shopper, the best
being the one who comes closest to $75 without
going over. You may want to work in teams.

There are only a few rules.
► You must buy at least one item from each of the
four categories.
► You can use each advertised price only once. For
example, if you see oranges advertised at 5 for
$0.99 you can buy 5 oranges, but no more than 5.
Also, you cannot buy fewer than 5 if they are
advertised at 5 for $0.99.

Meat/Fish		Fruits/Vegetables		Household Goods/Paper		Miscellaneous	
Item	Price	Item	Price	Item	Price	Item	Price

Name _____

Puzzle Challenges

Use the correct order of operations to solve each of these puzzles. Use each number or symbol in the puzzle once. You may move only between squares that are connected horizontally, vertically, or diagonally. A horizontal line in a square indicates subtraction.

What path would you follow to reach the number shown by the Exit sign?

1.

Enter

12	4	×
÷	+	6
2	–	5

Exit
25

2.

Enter

8	–	3
	2	×	+
Exit 6	4	÷	16

3. Where would you exit from this puzzle so that the result will be 17?

Enter

2	×	(
–	)	8
5	3	+

4. What number or symbol is needed to complete this puzzle?

	2^3	–	2
Enter	7	÷	+
Exit 33	?	×	6

5. How can you arrange these numbers and symbols in this puzzle so that the result will be 100?

7 28 8^2 10 4

+ – × ÷

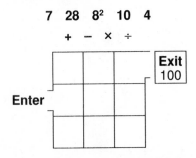

Exit 100

Enter

6. Use the frames below to create puzzles of your own.

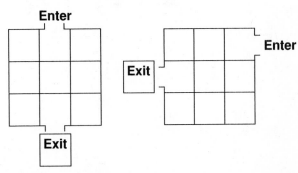

Enter

Exit

Enter

Exit

Name _____

Where Did the Dollar Go?

There is an old problem that has been puzzling math students for many years. See whether you can suggest a reasonable solution after reading it.

Where Did the Dollar Go?

Three travelers check into a hotel looking for an inexpensive place to sleep. The desk clerk informs them that the room will cost $30, whereupon each traveler hands the clerk $10. A short while later the bellhop knocks at their door. "The clerk made a mistake," says the bell hop. "The room should have been $25 not $30. He asked me to return $5 to you. The traveler who answered the door takes the five one-dollar bills, gives one to each of his companions, keeps one for himself, and gives the bellhop the other two as a tip. When the three men are alone again, they begin talking. "Something doesn't make sense," says one. "We each paid $10 at the desk. We each just got back one dollar. So the room cost us each $9 or a total of $27. We gave the bellhop $2. That makes $29. Where did the other dollar go?" Explain.

_____

_____

_____

_____

_____

_____

_____

_____

_____

_____

Name _____

For Sales

The pay scale charts for the ABC Appliance
Company and the XYZ Sound Systems are shown
below.

ABC Appliance Co.
$12 per hour
1.5 times $12 for hours over 25
8% for sales up to $3,000
12% for sales over $3,000

XYZ Sound Systems
$13.50 per hour
1.5 times $13.50 for hours over 35
6.5% for sales up to $1,500
10% for sales over $1,500

Make up a number of office hours and an amount of
sales for each salesperson. Then determine whether it
is better to work for ABC Appliance or XYZ Sound
Systems.

1. Susan Stroh

Office hours _____

Sales _____

ABC Appliance _____

XYZ Sound Systems _____

2. Betty Barrott

Office hours _____

Sales _____

ABC Appliance _____

XYZ Sound Systems _____

3. Joseph Justright

Office hours _____

Sales _____

ABC Appliance _____

XYZ Sound Systems _____

4. Aaron Albright

Office hours _____

Sales _____

ABC Appliance _____

XYZ Sound Systems _____

5. Michael Miller

Office hours _____

Sales _____

ABC Appliance _____

XYZ Sound Systems _____

6. Carol Carter

Office hours _____

Sales _____

ABC Appliance _____

XYZ Sound Systems _____

Name _____

Percent of Improvement

Pete Peterson recorded his home improvement expenses
for 7 years in this graph.

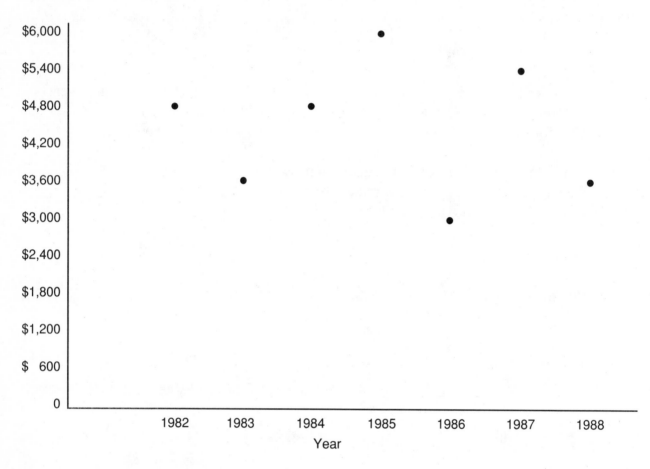

Pete wants to know the percent his expenses increased or decreased
from year to year. Complete the chart.

Year	1982	1983	1984	1985	1986	1987	1988
Expense	4,800	3,600					
Percent		⁻25%					

During what two-year period were Pete's expenses the greatest?
What was his percent of increase over the previous two-year period?

_____

Permill

35 per**cent** can be written as a fraction with a denominator of 100. The symbol for percent is %.

$$35\% = \frac{35}{100}$$

35 per**mill** can be written as a fraction with a denominator of 1,000. The symbol for permill is ‰.

$$35‰ = \frac{35}{1000}$$

Write each permill as a fraction in simplest form.

1. 200‰ _____

2. 50‰ _____

3. 500‰ _____

4. 25‰ _____

5. 750‰ _____

6. 80‰ _____

7. 400‰ _____

8. 5‰ _____

9. 20‰ _____

Write each as a decimal.

10. 200‰ _____

11. 50‰ _____

12. 80‰ _____

13. 405‰ _____

14. 1,000‰ _____

15. 325‰ _____

16. 5‰ _____

17. 10‰ _____

18. 67‰ _____

Solve. Use your calculator.

19. 300‰ of $90 _____

20. 15‰ of $1,000 _____

21. 60‰ of $120 _____

22. 250‰ of $500 _____

23. 2‰ of $1,200 _____

24. 100‰ of $40 _____

Name _____

Advertising Techniques

Form small groups to create an advertising campaign for a new type of bicycle. Decide on the propaganda techniques you will use. Write an advertisement for each of the following,

1. the local newspaper

2. a bicycle magazine

3. a radio station

4. a television program

Identify the type of propaganda that was used for each advertisement.

5. the local newspaper _____

6. a bicycle magazine _____

7. a radio station _____

8. a television program _____

Have several members of your group act out the advertisement for the television program.

Name _____

Writing Word Problems

You can write a new problem from a problem that
has already been written by

► changing the context/setting

► changing the numbers

► changing the conditions

► reversing the given and the wanted
information

► a combination of the above

Work in groups of four. Look at the problem
below. Then use any one of the principles above
to write a new problem for a friend to solve. An
example is given. Be sure you can solve your new
problem.

<table>
<tr><td>Original Problem</td><td>Change the Condition</td></tr>
<tr><td>There are chickens and pigs on Bob's farm. There are 18 animals in all. If you count the legs, you get 58. How many of each animal are there?</td><td>There are more pigs than chickens on Bob's farm. There are 18 animals in all. If you count the legs, you get 58. How many of each animal are there?</td></tr>
</table>

Now write your own variation.

1. _____

_____

_____

_____

2. _____

_____

_____

_____

3. _____

_____

_____

4. _____

_____

_____

Better Buy Now!

Use the information in the advertisements to predict the better buy. Then use a calculator to answer the questions.

Sue's Suits	
Blouses	$\frac{1}{2}$ off regular price $32 regular price
Skirts	20% off regular price $45 regular price
Jacket	15% off regular price $98 regular price

Carol's Clothes	
Blouses	40% off regular price $25 regular price
Skirts	25% off regular price $65 regular price
Jacket	$\frac{1}{5}$ off regular price $120 regular price

1. What is the sale price of a blouse at Carol's?

_____

2. What is the sale price of a skirt at Sue's?

_____

3. Which is the better buy, a jacket at Sue's or at Carol's?

_____

4. How much more does a skirt cost at Carol's than at Sue's?

_____

5. What is the regular price of a blouse, skirt, and jacket at Carol's?

_____

6. What is the sale price of an outfit at Sue's?

_____

CLOTHING SALE

Compound Interest

Interest is compounded if at the end of each time period the interest is added and the total amount becomes the principal. Today many bank accounts are compounded daily.

The formulas for simple interest are $I = P \cdot R \cdot T$ and $A = P + I$ where I is interest, P is principal, T is time, and A is amount.

The formula for compound interest is $A = P(I + R)^T$ where T is the time period.

For each problem below find the amount A and circle the larger amount. Use your calculator to help.

1. Simple Interest   Compounded Yearly   **2.** Simple Interest   Compounded Yearly

$P = \$1,000$	$P = \$500$	$P = \$2,500$	$P = \$2,500$
$R = 15\%$	$R = 15\%$	$R = 13\%$	$R = 13\%$
$T = 3$ years	$T = 3$ years	$T = 4$ years	$T = 4$ years
$A =$ _____	$A =$ _____	$A =$ _____	$A =$ _____

3. Simple Interest   Compounded Yearly   **4.** Simple Interest   Compounded Yearly

$P = \$800$	$P = \$800$	$P = \$600$	$P = \$600$
$R = 11\%$	$R = 10\%$	$R = 9\%$	$R = 8\%$
$T = 2$ years	$T = 2$ years	$T = 10$ years	$T = 9$ years
$A =$ _____	$A =$ _____	$A =$ _____	$A =$ _____

Name _____

Class Survey

Work in small groups. Take surveys in your class.
Select one student in the group as a record keeper
to count the votes and put the results on the board.
Copy the results here, and make circle graphs for
your surveys.

1. What is your favorite type of pet?

Selection	Number of Votes
dog	
cat	
bird	
fish	
other	

2. What is your favorite type of
television show?

Selection	Number of Votes
comedy	
soap opera	
drama	
game show	
other	

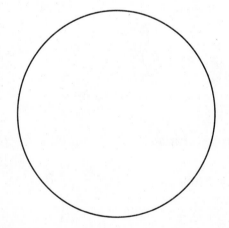

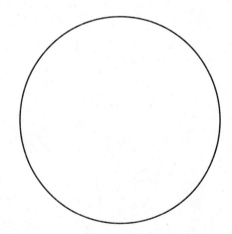

3. Make up a survey with your group. Have your
classmates respond, and make a circle graph of
your results.

Name _____

Food for Thought

Solve. If there is no solution, tell why. Then
change the condition of the problem so that it can
be solved. Give the rewritten problem to a friend
to solve. Check his or her answer.

1. The grocery store sells apples in 2-lb and 5-lb
bags. Jon bought 8 pounds of apples. How
many bags of each kind did he buy?

_____

_____

2. Aaron bought a box of strawberries at $1.79 a box,
oranges at 39¢ a pound, and a cantaloupe at $1.29.
He gave the clerk a $5 bill. How much change
did he receive?

_____

_____

3. Adena bought milk for $2.29 and a box of granola
bars for $1.79. She gave the clerk $4.50, and
received 6 coins for change. What coins did the
clerk give Adena?

_____

_____

4. Terry kept her weekly grocery receipts for one
month. She spent $104.35 the first week, $125.68
the second week, and $98.72 the third week.
What was her average weekly grocery bill for
the month?

_____

Name _____

Decisions, Decisions

Dear Family,
   We are studying the Basic Counting Principle. It tells us that we can find the total number of ways an event can happen by multiplying the number of choices at each step of the event. For example, suppose you have 3 pens and 7 pencils and want to make a drawing using a pen and a pencil. There are 3×7, or 21 possible pen and pencil combinations.
   Work together to estimate which of each pair of events would give you more choices. Then count the described items in your home and use the Basic Counting Principle to check your estimates.

Are there more choices when you:

1. Cook a dish using a saucepan and frying pan, or . . .

Choose a drink and fruit from the refrigerator?

2. Wash your hair with shampoo and conditioner, or . . .

Clean your car with car cleaner and wax?

3. Answer a ring of a doorbell and then a phone, or . . .

Take a nap on a bed, then on a sofa?

4. Take a walk wearing shoes, then wearing sneakers, or . . .

Take a car ride, then a bike ride?

Anagrams and Permutations

Anagrams are words or phrases made by
rearranging a given set of letters.

1. How many three-letter permutations can be
   made from the three letters at the right?

   | a | t | r |

   _____

2. List the permutations.

   _____

3. Ring the anagrams above.

4. How many four-letter permutations can be
   made from the four letters at the right?

   | g | s | a | h |

   _____

5. List the permutations. Then go back and ring
   the anagrams.

   _____

   _____

   _____

   _____

6. How many three-letter permutations can be
   made from the four letters at the right?

   | c | r | m | a |

   _____

7. List the permutations. Then go back and ring
   the anagrams.

   _____

   _____

   _____

   _____

8. Write your own anagram puzzle. Find four
   letters that form at least three anagrams. Give
   the puzzle to a friend to solve.

Horse Sense

There are many problems in mathematics based on someone's leaving something in a will to be divided fairly among relatives.

A horse farmer died and left his sons, Jed, Ned, and Ted all 17 of his horses. According to the will, the horses were to be divided as follows:

Jed was to get $\frac{1}{2}$ of them,

Ned was to get $\frac{1}{3}$ of them, and

Ted was to get $\frac{1}{9}$ of them.

17 horses to be shared, the brothers figured out that Jed would get $8\frac{1}{2}$ horses, Ned $5\frac{2}{3}$ horses, and Ted $1\frac{8}{9}$ horses. They realized that they had a serious problem.

Their cousin Fred offered to help. "Suppose I lend you one of my horses," suggested Fred. "Then you will have 18." With 18 you can do this:

"Jed gets $\frac{1}{2}$ of the 18, or 9 horses,

"Ned gets $\frac{1}{3}$ of the 18, or 6 horses, and

"Ted gets $\frac{1}{9}$ of the 18, or 2 horses.

"That adds up to 17. I take mine back and everyone is happy."

The brothers were amazed at Fred's horse sense, but were unable to figure out why his suggestion worked so perfectly. Can you?

_____

_____

_____

_____

_____

_____

Disguising The News

This is a school newpspaper article about the football game between Tamarack High School and its arch rival, Remington High. The only problem with the the article is that most of the numbers are written using factorial and exponential expressions instead of standard numerals. Interpret these expressions and substitute a standard numeral for each.

Tamarack High School was the setting on

Saturday, October 4! _____, of the county championship game between Tamarack and its cross-county rival, Remington High.

Attendance was 7! + 6! _____ people

with (6! • 5) + 89 _____ of that number being students. Remington quarterback Paul Douglas led his team to their first county title

in 3! _____ years by setting up 4 touchdown runs. The result was an impressive

2^2 • 7 _____ to 3! _____ victory.

Many records were broken during the game. The

5! – (4! + 8) _____ °F temperature was the hottest on record for this date. Refreshment stands reported a profit of 7! – (10^3 • 3) – 5!

_____ dollars, mostly due to the sale of fruit juices and ices. That is an increase of

6! + 10^2 + 55 _____ dollars over the profit at last years' game.

Remington High coach Ben Reed is looking

forward to next year. With 3! _____ starting players returning on each team, the next contest should be as exciting as this one.

Domino Sums

In a set of double-six dominoes, each domino has
two sides and each side has 0 to 6 pips.

1. In the space below, draw a complete set of
double-six dominoes.

Hint: This is the same as 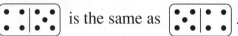.

2. How many dominoes are in a double-six set? _____

3. How many dominoes have a sum of 3? _____

4. How many dominoes have a sum of 10? _____

5. Which sums occur exactly twice? _____

6. Which sum is the most comon? _____

7. Which sums are the least common? _____

Name _____

Estimation

You can think of Pascal's triangle as a series of paths. Imagine removing the top pin of the triangle to open it up and dropping a marble in. Each number tells exactly how many paths there are through that opening.

For example:

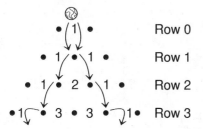
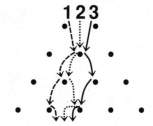

Each time the marble falls through an opening it hits the pin below. Each time it hits a pin, the marble has an even chance of falling to the left or right. Because of this you can count the number of paths there are to each opening. In row 3, there is only 1 way (shown in the picture) that the marble can reach either opening marked 1. However, there are 3 different paths the marble can take so that it falls through either opening marked 3. Try to find them.

Copy rows 0 through 3.

Use a colored pen or pencil to find the 3 different paths.

You can build this pinball machine yourself. You will need some tacks and a soft piece of wood or corkboard. Remember to make the space between all tacks the same and to space the tacks so that the marble hits a tack in each row.

Build the pinball machine with 6 rows first (rows 0-5).

1. How many different openings will be in row 5? _____

2. Which openings in row 5 have the most paths to them? How many?

_____

A Strange Inequality

Cut a square 8 centimeters on a side from centimeter graph paper. What is the area of the large square?

_____

Now label and cut the square into the four pieces shown here.

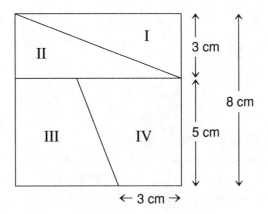

Rearrange the four pieces as shown below.

What are the length and width of the new rectangle?

_____

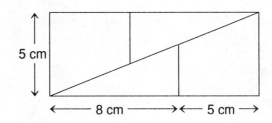

What is the area of the new rectangle?

_____

How can you explain the fact that the same pieces which originally had an area of 64 square centimeters now have an area of 65 square centimeters?

_____

_____

_____

Name _____

Advanced Tic-Tac-Toe

Dear Family,
     We are studying the use of problem-solving strategies in class. This game will help your teenager develop his or her strategy skills.

You may not have played this version of tic-tac-toe. The rules remain the same. Two players alternate, placing X's and O's on the board. The object of this game, however, is to place 4 marks in a row, not 3. The real change is the shape of the playing board. Rather than a 3 by 3 grid, play this version on a board of any randomly chosen shape. One example is shown below, but you may design the board to any shape you choose.

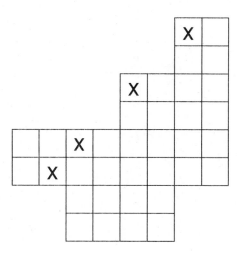

Variations:
In addition to or instead of 4 in a row, include 4 marks forming a square as a winning possibility.

As a real challenge, allow the 4 in a row to move off the board and then back on. In this version, the 4 X's marked on the board above would be a winner.

Strange Spinners?

Examine these spinners. An experiment with these spinners consists of spinning both and then adding the resulting numbers. The outcome for the experiment shown below is 7.

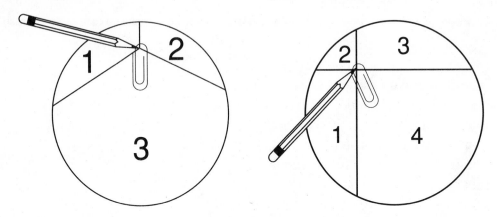

What is the sample space for this experiment? _____

If you were to spin both spinners 50 times, how many times do you think each outcome would occur? Fill in the table below.

Prediction	
Outcome _____ Number _____	Outcome _____ Number _____
Outcome _____ Number _____	Outcome _____ Number _____
Outcome _____ Number _____	Outcome _____ Number _____

Now do the experiment 50 times and keep a record of your results.
Make each spinner by first tracing it onto a sheet of unlined paper. Then straighten a paper clip to use as the arrow. Hold the paper clip in place with a pencil and your spinner is ready.

How do the results of your experiment compare with your predictions. Are these spinners

really strange? Explain _____

_____

Name _____

Probability Tables

Sometimes a table is helpful in listing all of the possible events.

1. This table shows the sums that are possible when both spinners are spun. Complete the table.

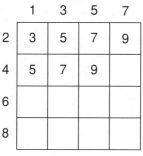

First spinner

Second spinner	1	3	5	7
2	3	5	7	9
4	5	7	9	
6				
8				

First spinner

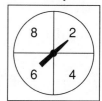

Second spinner

2. Which sums are the least probable?

_____

3. What is the probability of spinning a sum of 7?

_____

4. What is the probability of spinning a sum of 5 or 13?

_____

5. Complete the table showing the sums that are possible when two number cubes are thrown. Each cube is numbered 1 through 6.

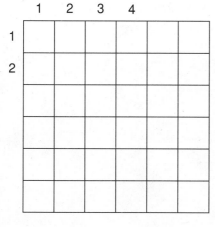

First cube

Second cube	1	2	3	4		
1						
2						

6. Which sum has the highest probability of being thrown?

_____

7. What is the probability of throwing a sum of 12?

_____

8. What is the probability of throwing a sum of 4?

_____

9. What is the probability of throwing a sum of 8, 9, or 10?

_____

Probability Experiment 1

You can make probability predictions based on your knowledge of geometry.

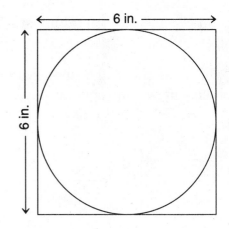

On a sheet of paper, draw a square that is 6 inches on each side. Find the center of the square. Now draw a circle inside the square so that the circle just touches each side of the square.

What is the area of the square? _____

What is the area of the circle rounded to the nearest

whole number? _____

What is the ratio of the area of the circle to the area

of the square? _____

Now make a prediction. If you drop a dime directly above the center of the square and circle, will it be more likely to land inside or outside the circle?

_____ If you do the experiment 100 times, how many times do you think the dime will land

inside the circle? _____

outside the circle? _____

Surround the square with books so that the dime cannot roll away. Count each outcome according to where most of the dime is lying. Work with a partner, one tossing and one recording. After 50 tosses, switch roles.

Are your results close to your prediction? _____

If not, what might explain the difference?

_____

_____

_____

Name _____

Fair Games?

Play each of these games with an opponent several times. Then answer each question for the game and the variation.

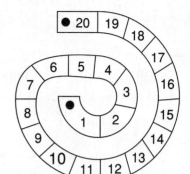

► Is the game fair?

► If not, who has the advantage?

1. Place markers on the 10. Player A must reach 1; Player B must reach 20. The first player rolls a number cube and moves the marker that number of spaces in his or her direction. The second player rolls the cube and moves the marker toward his or her goal. The first player to reach his or her goal wins.

_____

_____

Variation: Always allow Player B to go first.

_____

_____

2. Use the spinners with a pencil and a paper clip. Player A is "odd," Player B is "even." Spin both spinners. If the product is odd, A wins. If the product is even, B wins.

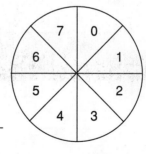 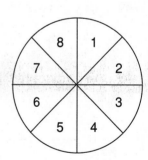

_____

_____

_____

Variation: If the product is odd, A gets 2 points. If the product is even, B gets 1 point. Player with most points after 20 rounds wins.

_____

Checkerboard Challenge

The kitchen floor in the picture has been tiled in a checkerboard pattern. One square has been removed from two corners to allow for pipes.

If each tile is one foot on each side, what is

the area of the kitchen? _____

The people who own this home have decided to retile the floor. The tiles they have chosen, unlike the ones now on the floor, are 2 feet long by 1 foot wide.

► Will it be possible to cover the floor completely without cutting any of the new tiles?

► If it is possible, what pattern will successfully cover the floor?

You can experiment by using an actual checkerboard and a cutout rectangle 2 squares by 1 square.

How can you explain your findings?

_____

_____

_____

_____

_____

_____

_____

_____

Probability Experiment

Make and label a spinner like the one at the right.

You can use the spinner with a pencil and paper clip.

A trial of this experiment consists of spinning the spinner, recording the outcome, spinning it again, and recording the outcome.

In conducting one trial, do you believe the outcome is more likely to be two spins of the same color or two spins of different colors?

Make a guess at the outcome for 50 trials:

    same color _____ + different colors _____ = 50

Conduct 50 trials of this experiment and record your results:

    same color _____ + different colors _____ = 50

Do the results surprise you?

To understand the explanation for these results, label each of the Blue sections Blue 1, Blue 2, and Blue 3. It does not matter in which order you label them.

Now list all the possible ways you can get two spins of the same color and two spins of different colors. In each list the first one has been filled in.

Spinner:

Blue	Blue
Blue	White

    Same color:

B1, B1; _____

    Different colors:

B1,W; _____

    How many possible outcomes are in the sample space of this experiment? _____

    What is the probability of two spins producing the same color? _____

    What is the probability of two spins producing a different color? _____

Raising Your Understanding of Sampling

Which do you think has more raisins: a snack-size box of raisins, a loaf of raisin bread, or a 15-ounce box of raisin bran cereal?

You could count the actual number of raisins in each, but that would be very time-consuming, not to mention messy. Or you could estimate the number in each by using a random sample.

Think about what would be a representative sample of the number of raisins in each.

► If you counted the number of raisins in a teaspoon, would it be a representative sample? By what number would you have to multiply them to estimate the number of raisins in a whole snack box?

_____

_____

► If you counted the number of raisins in a slice of raisin bread, would this be a representative sample of the raisins in the whole loaf? Why or why not?

_____

_____

How many slices of bread do you think would be a representative sample?

_____

► Would one cup of raisin bran cereal be a good sample for the number of raisins in a box of raisin bran? Why or why not? How many cups would you want to use?

_____

If you counted the number of raisins in a cup of raisin bran cereal, by what number would you have to multiply that amount in order to estimate the number of raisins in a whole box?

_____

Make a guess and then take samples of each. According to your sample, which of the three has more raisins?

_____

What can you conclude about the number of raisins you will find in any box of raisins, loaf of raisin bread, or box of raisin bran cereal?

_____

_____

Name _____

Expected Outcome

Among its many other uses, you can think of Pascal's triangle as a game board. Imagine the triangle standing upright. A marble is in one of the cups as shown at the right. If the marble lands in a W cup, the game owner pays you the number of dollars shown. If it lands in an L cup, you must pay the owner that amount.

Does this seem like a fair game? _____

You can decide whether it is fair by determining its *expected value*. This is the product of the probability of an event and the value of the event. For a game, first find the expected value of each possible outcome. Then add the expected values. A fair game will have an expected outcome of exactly 0, so if you played many times, you would win as much as you would lose.

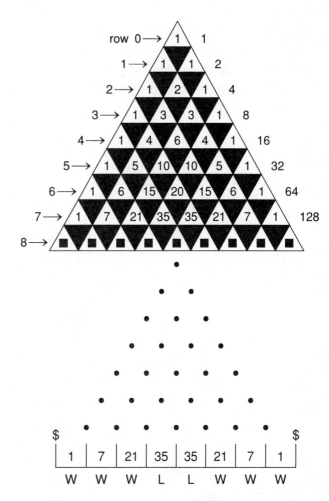

| 1 | 7 | 21 | 35 | 35 | 21 | 7 | 1 |
| W | W | W | L | L | W | W | W |

1. How many different paths are there *altogether* to the 8 cups? (Hint: Add the values in the bottom row.)

_____

2. Which numbers represent losses?

_____

Wins? _____

3. What amounts can you lose on each

play? _____

Wins? _____

4. What is the probability of each losing

event? _____

Of each winning event? _____

_____

You can determine the expected value (E):

$$E = \frac{1}{128} \times \$1(2) + \frac{7}{128} \times \$7(2) + \frac{21}{128} \times \$21(2) + \frac{35}{128} \times (^-\$35) \times 2 = {}^-\$11.47$$

This game has an expected value of $^-\$11.47$.

A Probability Mixed Bag

1. If a single card is drawn from a deck of 52 cards, what is the probability that the card will be:

a. a heart?

_____

b. not a heart?

_____

c. a 5 or a heart?

_____

d. a red picture card?

_____

e. a 5 or a 6

_____

f. a black card?

_____

g. a king or a jack?

_____

h. a queen?

_____

i. a prime number?

_____

j. an odd number?

_____

k. a 2-digit number?

_____

l. a perfect square?

_____

2. You have 3 quarters, 4 dimes, and 2 nickels in your pocket. If you choose a coin without looking, what is the probability that the coin is worth:

a. less than $0.25?

_____

b. less than $0.30?

_____

c. not more than $0.05?

_____

Name _____

A Finite Number System

An old riddle asks, "When does 9 + 5 = 2?" The answer is "on a clock." If you do not see that this is true, perhaps you are thinking of a digital clock. If you think of an analog clock (a regular clock on which all the numbers are visible), you will realize the 9 o'clock plus 5 hours brings you to 2 o'clock.

Unlike the decimal system, in which the numbers go on to infinity, a clock has a finite, or fixed, set of numbers. A clock is an example of a finite system with exactly 12 numbers. It is sometimes referred to as the modulo 12 system.

Other operations may also seem unusual in this system.

If you begin at 12 o'clock and take 3 consecutive 5-hour trips, at what time will you be finished?

Look at the table to answer the question.

Trip	Time Completed
1	5 o'clock
2	10 o'clock
3	3 o'clock

On the clock, 3 x 5 = 3.

Answer each of the questions for the modulo 12 system. Use the clock to help you.

1. 3 + 5 = _____ **2.** 8 + 4 = _____ **3.** 12 + 6 = _____ **4.** _____ + 9 = 3

5. 2 × 8 = _____ **6.** 5 × 12 = _____ **7.** 1 × 9 = _____ **8.** _____ × 2 = 2

9. 3 × _____ = 3 **10.** 12 − _____ = 9 **11.** 2 − _____ = 6 **12.** 3 − 7 = _____

Name _____

Polygons in Construction

For many centuries, engineers have known a vital fact about polygons: only one polygon is rigid. Once this polygon is constructed, its sides, unlike those of any other polygon, cannot be moved or shifted. You can experiment to discover which polygon has this attribute.

You will need: drinking straws, and pipe cleaners cut in thirds.

A pentagon is a good polygon with which to begin. Construct a pentagon by pushing a pipe cleaner piece into one end of a straw (fold the pipe cleaner in half, if necessary). Attach another straw to the remaining piece of pipe cleaner. Continue until your pentagon is complete. It will look like this:

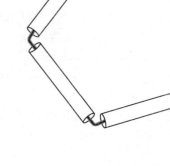

Can the pentagon be shifted to create a different

pentagon without detaching an of its sides: _____

Is it rigid? _____ Do you think you need to add

or remove sides to increase the rigidity? _____

Remove one side and construct a square. Is it

rigid? _____

Remove another side and construct a triangle.

Is it rigid? _____

Can you think of any applications in building construction that take advantage of this rigidity? _____

_____

_____

Pentominoe Puzzles

Dear Family,
    We are studying polygons made from pentominoes. This activity reinforces recognizing the different-shaped pentominoes.

Work together to fill in the blanks.

This diagram shows all 12 pentominoes. There are

_____ quadrilateral, _____ hexagons, _____

octagons, _____ decagons (10-sided polygon),

and _____ dodecagon (12-sided polygon).

The pentominoe polygons can be arranged in jigsaw puzzle fashion to create a large rectangle. Here's how: Copy the 12 pentominoes onto centimeter graph paper. Then cut out each one.

Use the rectangle below as a frame for your puzzle. More than one arrangement will work.

When you have solved this puzzle, create one of your own for a family member or friend to solve. Make sure to trace a frame for the puzzle. Without a frame, the puzzle is extremely difficult.

Name _____

Grid Area

This is the way Andrea found the area of the shaded figure.

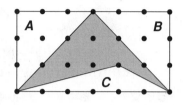

Area of whole grid: $3 \times 6 = 18$ square units

Area of triangle A: $\frac{1}{2} \times 3 \times 3 = 4.5$ square units

Area of triangle B: $\frac{1}{2} \times 3 \times 3 = 4.5$ square units

Area of triangle C: $\frac{1}{2} \times 6 \times 1 = 3$ square units

The total area of A, B, and $C = 4.5 + 4.5 + 3 = 12$ square units.
The area of the grid – the total area of A, B, and $C = 18 - 12 = 6$ square units.
The area of the shaded figure is 6 square units.

Find the area of each shaded figure.

1.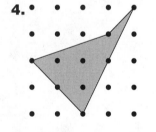
_____

2.
_____

3.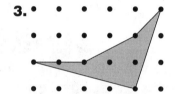
_____

4.
_____

5.
_____

6.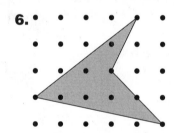
_____

7.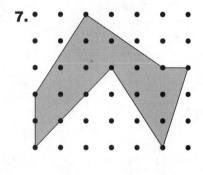
_____

8.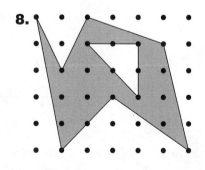
_____

An Ancient Art Form

Artists of ancient Persia developed the use of tessellations for decorating many of their buildings. One design that was used often was known as a star and cross pattern. You can easily re-create this pattern. With enough tiles, you can make a beautiful wall decoration.

To make the star: Cut a circle with a radius of 3 inches from an unlined sheet of paper.

Fold the circle in half, then in fourths, then in eighths, pizza style.

Lightly draw perpendicular lines from each lower corner to the opposite side. Cut to the point of intersection.

Unfold to see your 8-pointed star.

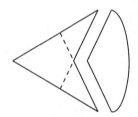

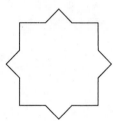

To make the cross: Begin with another 8-pointed star equal in size to the first.

Draw the following lines and cut out the 4 shaded squares …

to leave the cross.

Decorate the tiles any way you wish. Then begin your tessellation.

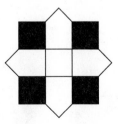

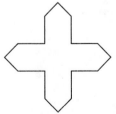

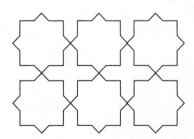

An X to a Square

The figure below can be cut along the indicated lines and reassembled to form the square. You can try this puzzle by tracing and cutting out the four pieces. Then use the square as a frame.

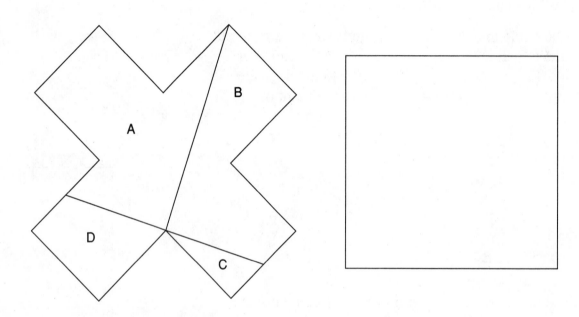

The length of each exterior line in the first figure is one inch.

What is the area of:

Section A? _____   Section B? _____

Section C? _____   Section D? _____

The entire figure? _____

The square? _____

Geometric Line Design

Follow these steps to make a line design in the space below.

Step 1 Use a compass to draw a circle with a radius of 6 cm.

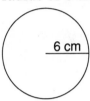

6 cm

Step 2 Leave the compass opening at 6 cm and mark six equal arcs around the circumference of the circle.

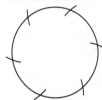

Start at any point on the circle.

Step 3 Connect the points to form a hexagon with six equilateral triangles inside.

Step 4 Use a ruler to mark every 0.5 cm as shown.

Step 5 Draw lines as shown in each triangle to make the design.

A Utilities Problem

Although we live in a 3-dimensional world, this problem requires you to think in only 2 dimensions.

A neighborhood is undergoing complete renovation. Part of the work consists of running new pipes for gas, electricity, and water to each house. The first street to be worked on contains only 3 houses. The houses and utilities stations are pictured below.

Is it possible to connect each of the houses to all 3 utilities in such a way that none of the lines crosses any other line? If it is possible, how can it be done?

Experiment until you believe you know the answer. How can you explain the solution?

_____

_____

_____

_____

Paper Folding II

Here is an activity that will help you see the
mathematics of an ellipse.

Draw a circle on a sheet of waxed paper.
Label the center of the circle O.

Choose another point anywhere inside the circle,
but not near point O. Label it P.

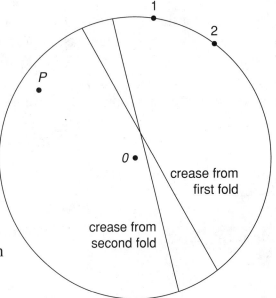

Fold the paper so that point P lies exactly on the
circle at point 1. Crease the waxed paper and open
it. Repeat for point 2.

Repeat the last step 20 times each time having
point P touch the circle at a different place.

Do you see the ellipse forming? When you see it.
try the following:

Label 2 points anywhere on the ellipse. Call them
E and F. Measure the following segments:

EO = _____   EP = _____   EO + EP = _____

FO = _____   FP = _____   FO + FP = _____

Now measure a radius of the circle. Call it R.

R = _____

What relationships do you notice?

_____

_____

_____

The Golden Triangle

The lengths of the sides of this triangle are related in a way that the ancient Greeks thought was pleasing to the eye. It is called a golden triangle.

Use the triangle for Problems 1 through 8.

1. m $\angle B$ = _____

2. m $\angle C$ = _____

3. $\overline{AB}$ = _____ cm

4. $\overline{AC}$ = _____ cm

5. $\overline{BC}$ = _____ cm

6. The length of $\overline{AB}$ divided by the length of $\overline{BC}$ rounded to the nearest thousandth is

_____ cm. This number should be close to the Golden Ratio, which is approximately 1.618.

7. Construct the bisector of $\angle ABC$.

8. Make the bisector of $\angle ABC$ intersect $\overline{AC}$. Name the intersection point D.

9. $\overline{BD}$ = _____ cm

$\overline{BC}$ = _____ cm

$\overline{DC}$ = _____ cm

10. The length of $\overline{BD}$ divided by the length of $\overline{DC}$ rounded to the nearest thousandth is

_____ cm

11. Is triangle *BDC* a golden triangle?

_____

A

B

C

Name _____

Balancing Triangles

You know how to balance a circle on a point — the center of the circle is the center of gravity. But how do you find the center of gravity of a triangle?
Experiment. Copy these triangles onto cardboard.

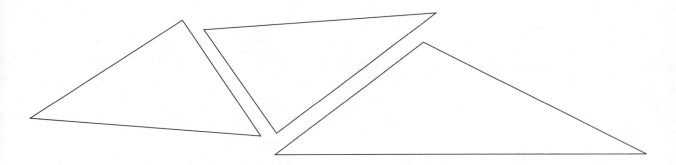

Place a dot on each triangle at the spot that you believe is the center of gravity. If you are correct, you should be able to balance the triangle at that point.

Test your guess. Cut out your triangles. Do they balance where you predicted they would? If not, here is a method for finding the center of gravity of any triangle.

Find the midpoint of each side.

Draw a line segment from each midpoint to the opposite vertex. Each of these segments is called a **median** of the triangle.

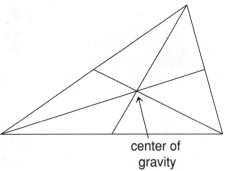

center of gravity

The point where the 3 medians intersect is the center of gravity.

The perpendicular bisectors of the sides of an obtuse triangle intersect outside the triangle. Can the medians of a triangle ever intersect outside the triangle?

If so, for what kind of triangle? _____

_____

_____

_____

Slicing Solids

Imagine slicing cleanly through the the cube as shown.
The cut surface of the cube that would be exposed
would be a rectangle.

What would the cut surface of the following solids look like?

 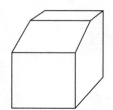 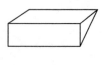

1.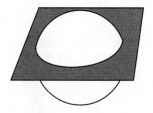

_____

2.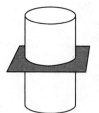

_____

3.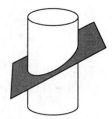

_____

4.

_____

5.

_____

6.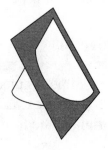

_____

7.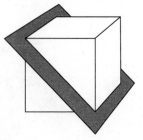

_____

8.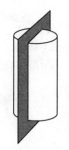

_____

9.

_____

The Wonderful World of 9

Look at each row of examples. Write another example that displays the same pattern. Then describe the pattern.

1. A

$$\begin{array}{r} 785 \\ -\ 587 \\ \hline 198 \end{array}$$

$198 \div 9 = 22$

B

$$\begin{array}{r} 8{,}604 \\ -\ 4{,}068 \\ \hline 4{,}536 \end{array}$$

$4{,}536 \div 9 = 504$

C

$$\begin{array}{r} 7{,}611 \\ -\ 1{,}167 \\ \hline 6{,}444 \end{array}$$

$6{,}444 \div 9 = 716$

D _____

_____

_____

2. A

$$\begin{array}{r} 17 \\ \times\ 9 \\ \hline 153 \end{array}$$

$1 + 5 + 3 = 9$

B

$$\begin{array}{r} 382 \\ \times\ 9 \\ \hline 3{,}438 \end{array}$$

$3 + 4 + 3 + 8 = 18$
$1 + 8 = 9$

C

$$\begin{array}{r} 8{,}501 \\ \times\ 9 \\ \hline 76{,}509 \end{array}$$

$7 + 6 + 5 + 0 + 9 = 27$
$2 + 7 = 9$

D _____

_____

_____

3. A

$$\begin{array}{r} 123 \\ -\ (1 + 2 + 3) \\ \hline 117 \end{array}$$

$117 \div 9 = 13$

B

$$\begin{array}{r} 2{,}147 \\ -\ (2 + 1 + 4 + 7) \\ \hline 2{,}133 \end{array}$$

$2{,}133 \div 9 = 237$

C

$$\begin{array}{r} 6{,}023 \\ -\ (6 + 0 + 2 + 3) \\ \hline 6{,}012 \end{array}$$

$6{,}012 \div 9 = 668$

D _____

_____

_____

Egyptian Numerals

Dear Family,
    We are studying square roots in class. This activity provides an opportunity to practice finding square roots while decoding ancient Egyptian numerals.

The ancient Egyptians had a base 10 numeral system.
Their system used symbols to represent powers of 10.
Among the symbols they used were these:

Coiled rope	Bent finger	Heel mark	Stroke	Lotus flower

These symbols represented 100, 1,000, 10, 1, and 10,000, but not in that order.
Use the following clues to determine which symbol represented which number.

1. $\sqrt{\text{((} \math{\mskip} \text{∩∩|||||}} = \text{⑨∩∩∩∩|||||}$

2. $\sqrt{\text{⑨∩∩∩∩∩||||||}} = \text{∩∩∩||||}$

3. $\sqrt{\text{(⑨⑨⑨⑨∩∩||||||}} = \text{⑨||||||||}$

⑨ = _____ (= _____ ∩ = _____ | = _____ = _____

Write the answers to the following using Egyptian numerals. Between which two whole numbers is:

4. $\sqrt{\text{⑨⑨∩∩∩|}}$? Between _____ and _____

5. $\sqrt{\text{(∩||||}}$? Between _____ and _____

6. $\sqrt{\text{⑨⑨⑨⑨|||}}$? Between _____ and _____

7. $\sqrt{\text{∩∩}}$? Between _____ and _____

8. $\sqrt{\text{(((⑨⑨∩∩∩∩|||}}$? Between _____ and _____

Estimating the Value of Pi

One of the most interesting numbers, one that has fascinated mathemeticians for centuries, is pi (π). This irrational number expresses the relationship between the circumference of any circle and its diameter. You can multiply the diameter of any circle by pi (3.14159 . . .) to find the circumference.

There are many experiments having nothing to do with circles that involve estimating the value of pi. Here is one you can easily try with a partner.

On a sheet of unlined paper, mark off straight lines equally spaced. Make the distance between the lines approximately 2 inches.

Break off 10 one-inch pieces from toothpicks.

Drop the toothpicks onto the paper from a height of about a foot.

Record the number of toothpicks that either cross or touch a line.

Keep a table for 50 tosses (a total of 500 toothpicks dropped).

Finally, simplify this fraction:

$$\frac{\text{Number of toothpicks dropped (in this case 500)}}{\text{Number crossing or touching a line}}$$

This should give you a value approximately equal to pi. Does it? Keep in mind that this is an experiment in probability. The more times you perform the experiment, the closer to pi your results will be.

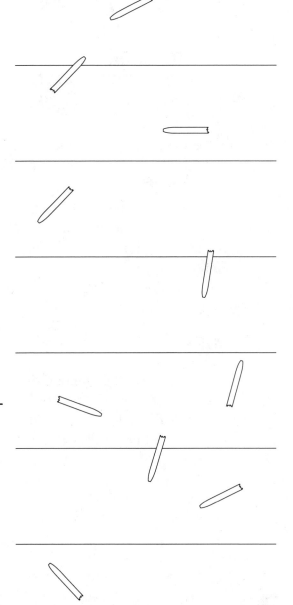

Inequality Logic

> Dear Family,
>   We are studying inequalities in class. Here are several logic puzzles that use the idea of inequalities in their solution.

1. Alpha, Beta, Gamma, and Delta are dogs belonging to the Omega family. The Omegas wanted to rank the dogs from lightest to heaviest. They used a balance scale 3 times. This is what they found:

Rank the Omegas' dogs from lightest to heaviest:

_____ , _____ , _____ , _____

2. A jewelry store owner had 5 valuable stones: a diamond, an emerald, a pearl, a ruby, and a sapphire. Each stone had a different value. Use these facts about the stones' values to order them from least valuable to most valuable:

The diamond and emerald together are worth less than the ruby. The diamond is worth more than the emerald and the pearl together. Only the sapphire is between the diamond and ruby in value. The pearl is worth less than the emerald.

_____ , _____ ,

_____ , _____ ,

_____

3. The Counterfeit Billiard Ball Detecting Agency (the CBBDA) uses a balance scale to detect phony billiard balls. A phony billiard ball weighs slightly less than a genuine one. The CBBDA has 9 billiard balls to weigh: 8 genuine and 1 counterfeit. How can they determine the counterfeit one by using the balance scale only twice?

_____

_____

_____

_____

_____

_____

_____

_____

Fish, Movies, and Jeans

1. Harold lives in Oregon and doesn't like to eat
fish. He knows that fish is easy to buy in Oregon
because it borders the Pacific Ocean.
He knows that Kansas is not near an ocean.
Thus he wants to convince his parents to move
to Kansas so they will not be able to buy fish.
In Kansas, Harold feels he will not have to eat fish.
What is wrong with his reasoning?

_____

_____

2. Mr. Hill has been the manager at the Spree
Movie Theater for over 15 years. He is
extremely patient and kind to all the
customers. One day a teenager was thrown out
of the theater for misbehaving and told never to
return. The teenager was a frequent moviegoer.
Do you feel the teenager had really been
disruptive? Or do you feel Mr. Hill just had a bad
day? Justify your answer.

_____

_____

3. Sara needed new jeans. At school her friends
told her not to go to the Blues Store in the mall
because the clerks were rude and unhappy. They
suggested she buy her jeans at the Great Slax
Store, another store in the mall. When Sara got
to the mall, she noticed that the Blues Store had
her favorite brand of jeans on sale at 30% off.
Where do you think Sara should buy her jeans?

_____

_____

Name _____

Sporting Distances

Find the distance each ball will travel from point
A to point *B*. Use a calculator. Round to the
nearest hundredth.

1. Baseball Diamond

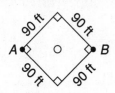

_____

2. Football Field

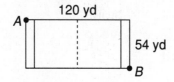

_____

3. Basketball Court

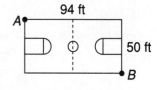

_____

4. Soccer Field

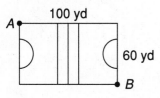

_____

5. Softball Diamond

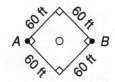

_____

6. Tennis Court

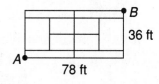

_____

The swimming pools below are missing the length
of one side. Find the length using a calculator.
Round to the nearest hundredth.

7.

_____

8.

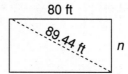

_____

9.

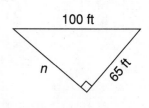

_____

Solve. Round to the nearest hundredth.

10. A badminton court is a rectangle
17 ft by 44 ft. What is the minimum
distance that a shuttle can travel from
one corner to the other?

_____

11. A Ping-Pong table is 9 ft long. If the
diagonal measures 10.3 ft, how wide
is the table?

_____

Name _____

Unusual Packaging Problems

A department store uses the following test to see whether job applicants in its wrapping department have what it takes. Would you qualify?

1. Would a $3\frac{1}{2}$-foot long umbrella fit into this carton?

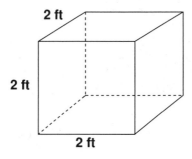

2 ft

2 ft

2 ft

_____

_____

_____

2. What is the longest umbrella that would fit into this carton?

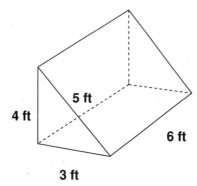

5 ft

4 ft

6 ft

3 ft

_____

_____

Name _____

Pick's Theorem

You have found the area of a variety of polygons using formulas. Since 1899, however, an unusual formula has existed for finding the area of geoboard or dot paper polygons. In that year, George Pick discovered this theorem:

$$\text{Area} = I + B/2 - 1$$

where I is the number of pegs or dots **inside** the polygon and B is the number of pegs or dots on the **boundary** or perimeter of the polygon.

Use Pick's theorem to find the area of each of these polygons. Then find the area another way. Do the results always match?
(If done accurately, they should.)

1.

A = _____

2.

A = _____

3.

A = _____

4.

A = _____

5.

A = _____

6.

A = _____

Use with text pages 406–407.

Name _____

A New Geometry

The geometry that we study is largely based on plane or flat surfaces. There is another branch of geometry, however, that follows a different set of principles, with some surprising results. You can think of this branch as spherical geometry. The earth is a good model for spherical geometry. Here are some ideas from this field.

There are no parallel lines on a sphere.
This will be true only if the term *line* is defined as a *"great circle."* A great circle is a line around the sphere whose intersection with the sphere passes through the sphere's center. All longitude lines on the earth are great circles. What is the only latitude line that is a great circle?

_____

A triangle must have an angle sum of more than 180°.
Look at the drawing. If the sides of a triangle are parts of great circles, a spherical triangle will have at least 2 right angles. What is the sum of the angles in this spherical triangle?

_____

Can you sketch a spherical triangle with an angle sum of less than the one pictured?

More?_____

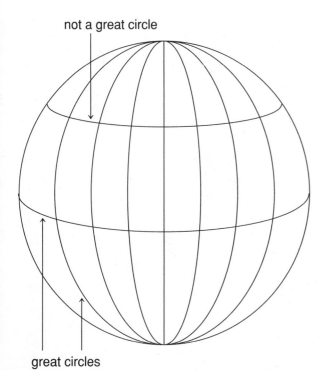

not a great circle

great circles

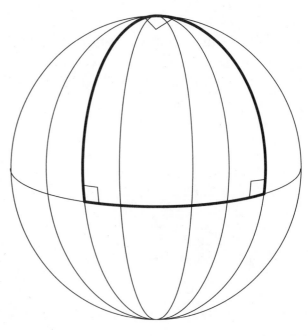

Name _____

Diagonal Distances

Solve using your calculator. Use any problem
solving strategy. Round answers to the nearest
tenth. All street intersections are at right angles.

1. Pedro is standing at the corner of Elm
St. and West St. If he walks diagonally
to the corner of East St. and Oak St.,
how far will he walk?

_____

2. Bryan walked diagonally from the
corner of Elm St. and West St. to the
corner of Maple St. and East St. How
far did he walk?

_____

3. How much farther did Bryan walk
than Pedro?

_____

4. The diagonal distance from the corner
of Maple St. and West St. to the corner
of Birch St. and East St. is 700 feet.
What is the distance from the corner
of Maple St. and East St. to the corner
of Birch St. and East St.?

_____

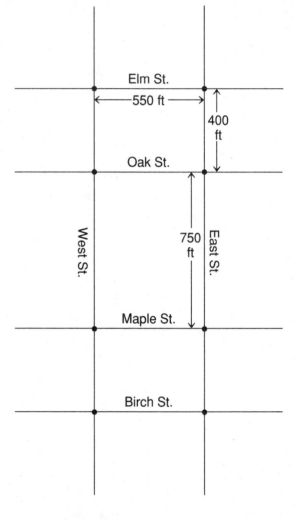

5. What is the distance from the corner
of Birch St. and East St. to the corner
of West St. and Oak St.?

_____

6. Find the distance from the corner of
Elm St. and West St. to the corner of
Birch St. and East St.

_____

7. If all your answers are correct, the sum
should be 5,963. What should you do if

your sum does not match? _____

_____

Sliding Your Way Home

Poor you! You have been dropped off far from
home (at the You Are Here sign) and left alone.
Well, almost alone. You do have a set of six slide
(translation) arrows which, if placed properly end
to end, will lead you directly to your front door.

Can you discover the arrangement that will lead you home?

Is there more than one possible arrangement? _____

How can you explain your findings? _____

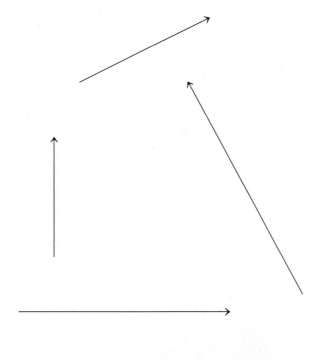

Your
Front Door

You
Are Here

Reflection Challenges

1. Draw the reflection image of parallelogram *QRST* after a
reflection in line *a* followed by a reflection in line *b*.

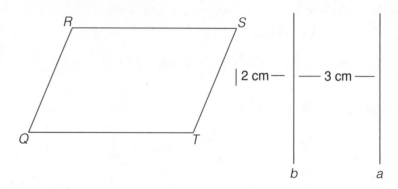

What single translation would be equivalent to the two

reflections described above? _____

2. Draw two lines, *a* and *b*, so that the shaded figure is the
image of the clear figure after a reflection over *a* followed
by a reflection over *b*.

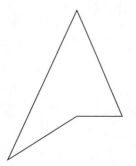

Finding Turn Centers

You can find the turn center for certain rotations by following these steps:

► Connect two original points to their image points with line segments, such as *A* to *A′* and *B* to *B′*.

► Draw the perpendicular bisectors of segments *AA′* and *BB′*.

► The point where the perpendicular bisectors intersect is the turn center.

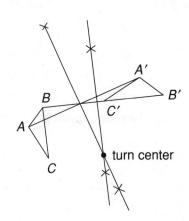

Find the turn centers for these rotations.

1.

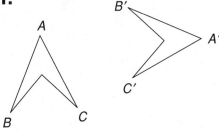

2.

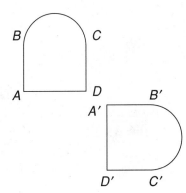

3.

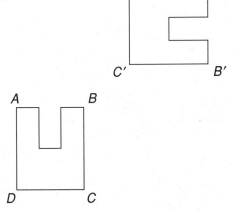

4.

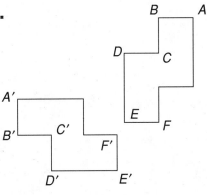

Why are two perpendicular bisectors sufficient?

_____

A Symmetrical Game

Dear Family,
   We are studying symmetry in class. Here is a game in which a winning strategy is based on using the notion of symmetry.

Construct a board like the one drawn here.

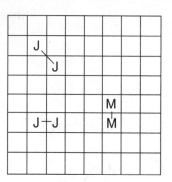

Players alternate claiming two adjoining squares by placing their initials in them and connecting them with a line. The squares you claim on one move may, as shown in the picture, touch horizontally, vertically, or diagonally.

You may not claim squares that would force your line to cross an already existing one.

The player who is able to claim the last two squares is the winner.

Explain how symmetry is involved in a winning strategy.

_____

_____

_____

_____

_____

_____

A Polygon Puzzle

Dear Family,
    We have been studying polygons. Here is a chance to work together on a polygon puzzle.

Five pairs of congruent figures can fit together to form a square that is 12 cm on a side. Draw a square with sides of 12 cm on cm graph paper to use as a frame for the puzzle. Cut out each figure and a second one congruent to it. Then use the clues to help determine the placement of the pieces.

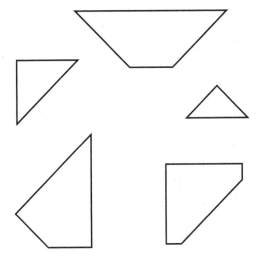

1. The trapezoids touch each other and are reflection images of each other. The reflection line is the shortest side of the trapezoid.

2. The pentagons are reflection images of each other. The reflection line is one of the lines of symmetry of the figure formed by the two trapezoids.

3. The quadrilaterals are rotation images of each other. The rotation is a $\frac{1}{2}$ turn around the center point of the puzzle.

4. The small triangles are also rotation images of each other. Both the size of the turn and its center point are the same as for the quadrilaterals.

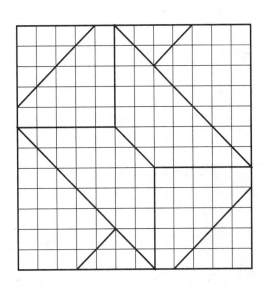

5. The large triangles touch opposite corners of the puzzle. They are both reflection images and turn images of each other.

Name _____

Corporate Trademarks

Figures with symmetry, either reflectional or rotational, are pleasing to the eye. Because of this, many companies use figures with symmetry for their logos or trademarks.

Look through newspapers, magazines, and catalogs for logos or trademarks. Use a mirror to decide on the number of lines of symmetry in each. Then sketch, trace, or cut out and paste to complete the chart.

Trademarks or Logos with . . .

No lines of symmetry			
Exactly one line of symmetry			
Exactly two lines of symmetry			
More than two lines of symmetry			
Rotational symmetry			

Hidden Equation

Play this game against one opponent.

Write a simple equation such as $y = x + 6$ or $y = 2x + 3$ without letting your opponent see it.

Take turns naming points on the grid. For each point named, the opponent must answer either "hit" or "miss."

► Hit indicates that the point named is on the graph of the equation.

► Miss indicates that the point named is not on the graph of the equation.

Continue naming points until you think you can identify your opponent's equation. The first person who correctly identifies his or her opponent's equation wins.

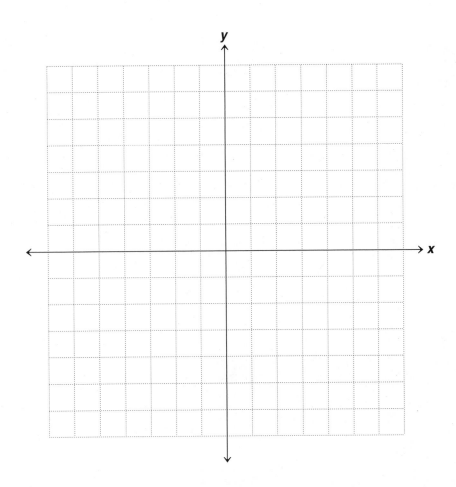

Use with text pages 432–433.

A Handshake Variation

The X's inside each circle represent a group of friends. Within each group, the friends would like to shake hands with exactly 3 other friends. A line drawn between 2 friends represents one handshake. Try to draw lines from each friend to exactly 3 others. The lines may cross and do not have to be straight. Decide if it is possible or impossible.

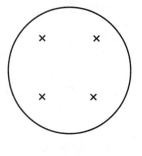

_____

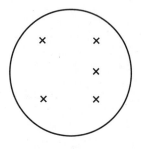

_____

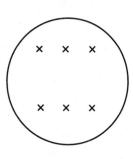

_____

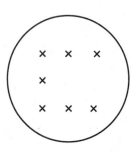

_____

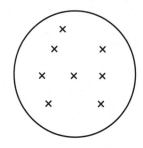

_____

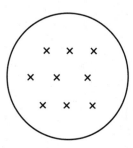

_____

What pattern do you see? _____

_____

_____

Explain why this pattern exists. _____

_____

_____

Congruent Segments

For several thousand years, since the time of the ancient Greeks, an apparently simple problem had frustrated mathematicians: How can you trisect an angle (divide it into 3 equal parts) using only a compass and an unmarked straight edge? Many "solutions" to this problem were proposed, but not until the 19th century was it proved that a solution was impossible.

For at least as long, however, mathematicians have known how to trisect a line segment. In fact, the procedure described below can be used to divide any segment into as many congruent parts as you wish.

To trisect segment $\overline{AB}$:

A ———————————————— B

▶ Draw $\overline{AC}$, making any $\angle BAC$.

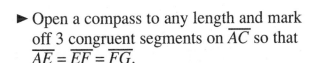

▶ Open a compass to any length and mark off 3 congruent segments on $\overline{AC}$ so that $\overline{AE} = \overline{EF} = \overline{FG}$.

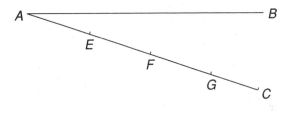

▶ Draw $\overline{GB}$. Then construct $\overline{FH}$ and $\overline{EJ}$, both parallel to $\overline{GB}$.

$\overline{AJ} = \overline{JH} = \overline{HB}$

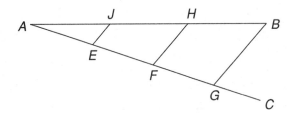

Use this method to divide these segments into the given number of parts. First copy them onto a separate sheet of paper.

_____   _____

5   4

Is SSS Enough?

Cut drinking straws or thin strips of paper the
length of each line segment shown at the right.
Then arrange them to form a triangle.

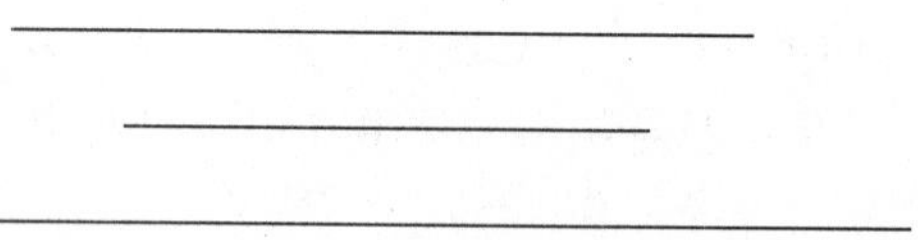

Compare your triangle with those of at least three

other students. Are all the triangles congruent to

one another? _____

Repeat the activity for each set of segments,
forming either a triangle or quadrilateral as
appropriate. In each case compare your polygon
to those of at least three others.

1.

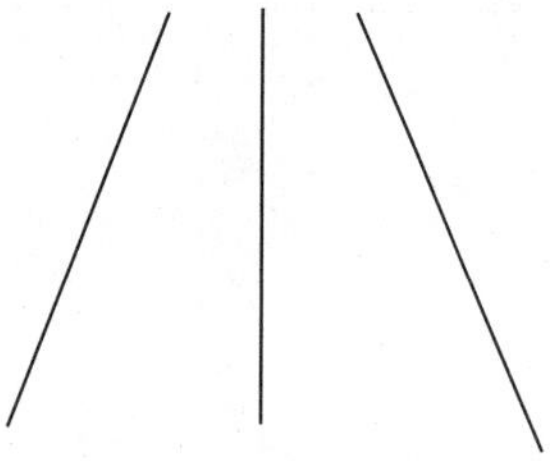

2.

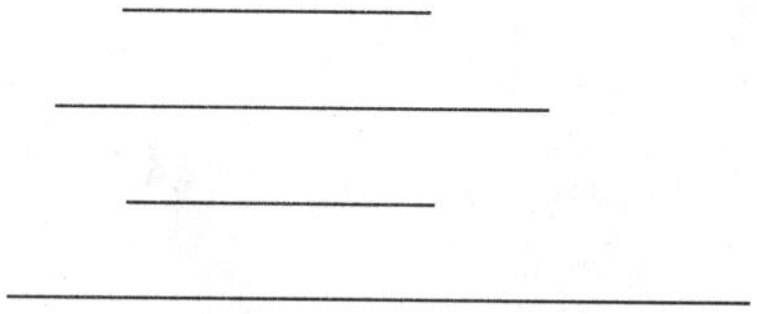

3.

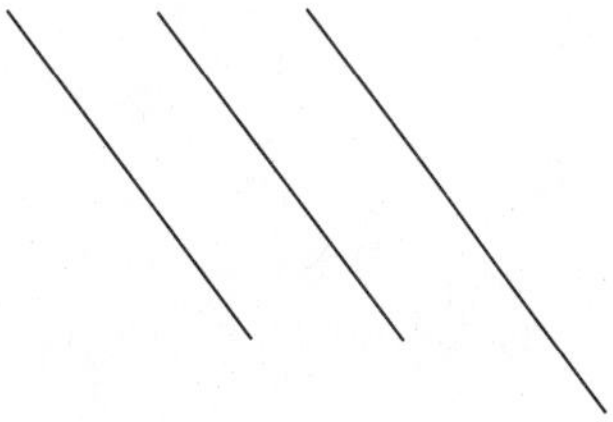

4.

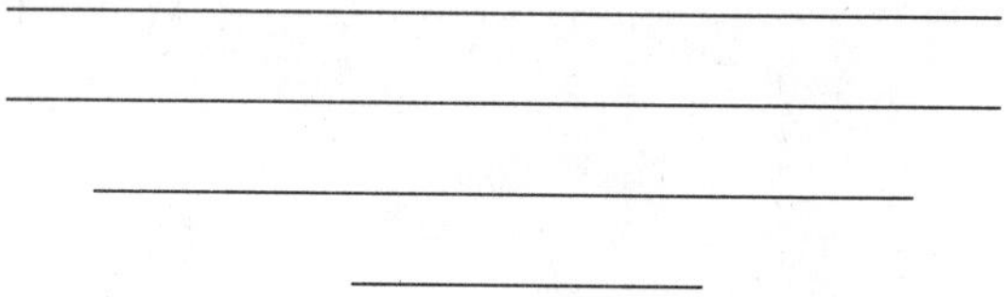

5.

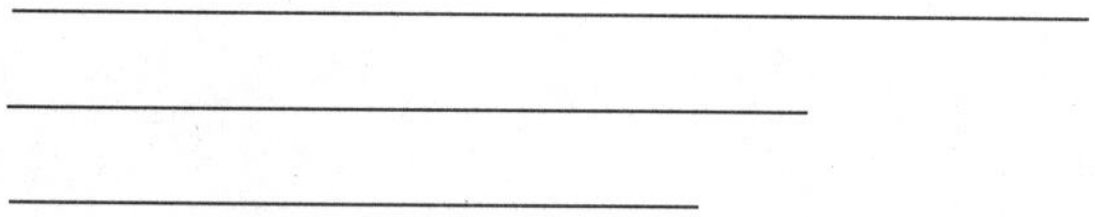

6.

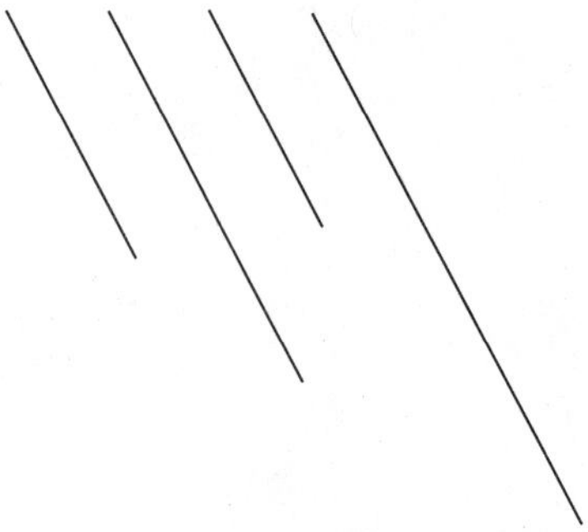

What conclusion can you draw? _____

_____

_____

Congruent Triangle Hunt

Grids B and C are distortions of grid A. The 3 grids contain 5 sets of triangles that were congruent before B and C were distorted.

Fill in the chart below by identifying the sets of congruent figures.

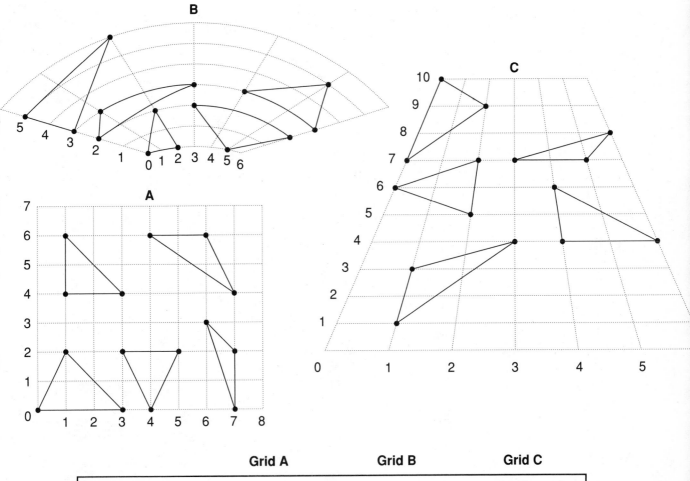

	Grid A	Grid B	Grid C
Set 1			
Set 2			
Set 3			
Set 4			
Set 5			

Consecutive Number Sums

The number 30 can be written as the sum of consecutive numbers.

$$30 = 5 \times 6 = 6 + 6 + 6 + 6 + 6 = 4 + 5 + 6 + 7 + 8$$

The number 45 can also be written as the sum of consecutive numbers.

$$45 = 3 \times 15 = 15 + 15 + 15 = 14 + 15 + 16$$

Experiment to find which of the following numbers can be written as the sum of consecutive numbers. Use only positive integers. Find the rule that explains the pattern.

1. 20 _____

2. 27 _____

3. 50 _____

4. 48 _____

5. 64 _____

6. 16 _____

7. 72 _____

8. 32 _____

What pattern do you notice? _____

_____

Series Sense

Dear Family,
    We have been studying number patterns. This game provides practice in estimating sums of number sequences, a skill related to understanding patterns. Play the game with 2 or 3 players.

► Each player writes an estimate for the sum of the first series.

► Use a calculator or formula to determine the exact sum.

► The player with the closest estimate wins the round and scores one point.

► At the end of 10 rounds, the player with the most points wins the game.

1. $17 + 18 + 19 + 20 + 21 + 22 + 23 =$ _____

2. $1 + 3 + 5 + 7 + 9 + 11 + 13 + 15 =$ _____

3. $1 + 4 + 7 + 10 + 13 + 16 + 19 + 22 =$ _____

4. $2 + 6 + 10 + 14 + 18 + 22 + 26 =$ _____

5. $51 + 52 + 53 + 54 + 55 + 56 + 57 + 58 + 59 + 60 =$ _____

6. $20 + 22 + 24 + 26 + 28 + 30 + 32 + 34 =$ _____

7. $1 \times 2 \times 3 \times 4 \times 5 \times 6 =$ _____

8. $20 + 19 + 18 + 17 + 16 + 15 =$ _____

9. $16 + 20 + 24 + 28 + 32 + 36 + 40 + 44 =$ _____

10. $98 + 97 + 96 + 95 + 94 + 93 + 92 + 91 + 90 =$ _____

Similar Figures

You would like to use tiles in the shapes below for an art project. You want to use the tiles to make figures similar to the ones you see. Can you make a figure similar to the one you see from the exact number of tiles you have? If not, how many tiles would make the largest possible similar figure? How many would you have left?

For example, if you had 5 rectangular tiles, you could make a similar figure using 4 of the tiles. You would have 1 left over.

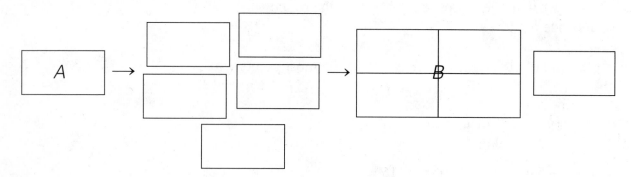

Rectangles *A* and *B* are similar.

In each case, write the largest number of tiles you can use to make a similar figure. If you cannot make a similar figure regardless of how many tiles you use, write *impossible*.

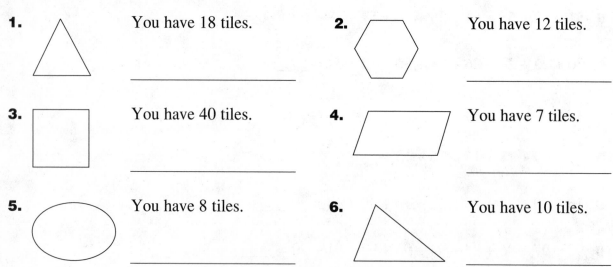

1. You have 18 tiles.

_____

2. You have 12 tiles.

_____

3. You have 40 tiles.

_____

4. You have 7 tiles.

_____

5. You have 8 tiles.

_____

6. You have 10 tiles.

_____

Fibonacci and Pascal: Colleagues?

You have examined the Fibonacci series of numbers:

1, 1, 2, 3, 5, 8, 13, 21, 34, 55, 89 . . .

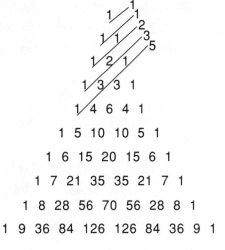

You have also worked with Pascal's triangle, finding patterns.

Are the two related? Can you find one in the other?

Try this.

```
            1
          1   1
        1   2   1
      1   3   3   1
    1   4   6   4   1
  1   5  10  10   5   1
1   6  15  20  15   6   1
1   7  21  35  35  21   7   1
1   8  28  56  70  56  28   8   1
1   9  36  84 126 126  84  36   9   1
```

▶ Draw the first 10 rows of Pascal's triangle.

▶ Draw the first 5 diagonals shown and write the totals along the diagonals.

▶ Continue drawing diagonals parallel to the ones already seen. Add along each diagonal and write the total.

▶ Do you see the Fibonacci series emerging?

Could Fibonacci and Pascal have worked together in developing these patterns? Look up both men in an encyclopedia. What do you find?

_____

_____

_____

_____

_____

_____

_____

_____

Attribute Sets

Work with a partner to make a set of attribute shapes. Cut the following figures from colored construction paper. For each figure, cut one from red, one from yellow, and one from blue paper:

3 squares 2 in. on a side   3 squares 1 in. on a side
3 triangles 2 in. on a side   3 triangles 1 in. on a side
3 rectangles 3 in. by 2 in.   3 rectangles 2 in. by 1 in.

Make 3 large loops from string. Use the attribute shapes to complete each of these diagrams.

1.
     Squares   Red

2.
     Blue   Rectangles

3.
     Not Small   Yellow

4.
     Not Red   Not Large

5.
    Triangles   Blue
Triangles   Blue
                Large
Large

6.
    Not Large   Yellow
Not Large   Yellow
               Not Rectangles
Not Rectangles

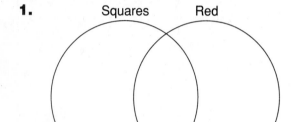
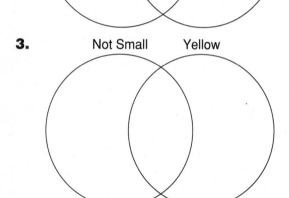
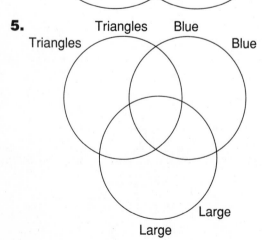
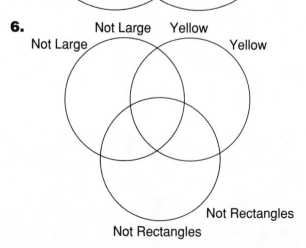

The 15-Puzzle Box

This puzzle, with which you may be familiar, was invented in the 19th century. For a number of years after its invention it was extremely popular.

1	2	3	4
5	6	7	8
9	10	11	12
13	14	15	■

The object of the puzzle is to slide the numbers into a desired position from any starting position. Because there are 16 spaces including the empty one, there are 16! or 20,922,789,888,000 possible arrangements. However, not all of them can be accomplished. Mathematicians have discovered a means of determining whether a position is possible.

Anytime a number precedes a number smaller than itself, call it a *reversal*. In the puzzle shown here, there are the following reversals:

4	1	2	3
7	5	6	8
9	10	12	11
13	14	15	■

4 precedes 1, 2, and 3 = 3	(3 reversals)
7 precedes 5 and 6 = 2	(2 reversals)
12 precedes 11 = +1	(1 reversal)
___	
6	

There are 3 + 2 + 1 = 6 reversals

If the sum of the reversals is **even**, the position is possible.

If the sum of the reversals is **odd**, the position is impossible.

Are these positions possible?

1.

1	2	■	3
7	6	5	4
8	9	10	11
15	14	13	12

2.

1	2	3	4
5	■	6	7
8	11	10	9
12	13	14	15

3.

2	4	7	1
6	3	5	9
10	■	11	15
12	8	14	13

_____   _____   _____

Name _____

Travel Routes

The recently uncovered ancient city of
Mathedonia was discovered to have a grid
of one-way streets, all heading east or
south (apparently no one ever returned
home once he or she left).

Suppose a Mathedonian wanted to travel
from the northwest corner of town to the
southeast corner. How many streets long
would the shortest route be?

_____

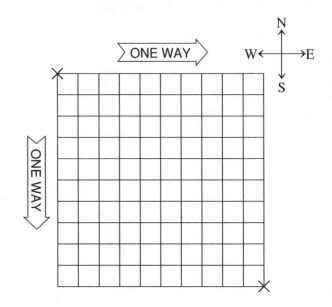

Determine the number of different routes
of the same length that are possible for the
trip described above. Choose a strategy.
(Hint: First find the number of routes to
closer destinations. You may begin to
recognize a familiar number pattern.)

If you treat the grid as Pascal's triangle and
compute the number of routes to closer
destinations, the pattern begins to emerge:

	1		1		1
1	2				
			3		4
1		3	6		10
					1
1		4	10		20

Now answer the question: How many
routes of the same length are possible for
the Mathedonian's trip described above?

_____

When Is Labor Day?

How many days each year does the "average" American work? Not very many, at least according to this way of counting:

Number of days in a year	365 days
Eight hours' sleep each night	– 122 days
	243 days
Eight nonworking hours each day	– 122 days
	121 days
Fifty-two Sundays each year	– 52 days
	69 days
Fifty-two Saturdays each year	– 52 days
	17 days
Two weeks' vacation	– 14 days
	3 days

Does the average American work only 3 days per year?

Does this chart make sense? _____

What inconsistencies do you see? What duplications?

_____

_____

_____

_____

Area and Perimeter Relationships

Dear Family,
    We are studying the use of logical reasoning in geometry. This activity encourages the use of logical reasoning in deciding on perimeter and area relationships.

Do perimeter and area always move in the same direction? That is, if you increase a figure's perimeter, must the area increase? If you shrink the perimeter, must the area also shrink?

Experiment with the figure below. Then answer the questions.

Area = _____

Perimeter = _____

Can you change the figure to one with:

The same area and a larger perimeter?
Area = 17 square units

Perimeter = _____

The same area and a smaller perimeter?
Area = 17 square units

Perimeter = _____

The same perimeter and a larger area?
Perimeter = 20 units

Area = _____

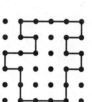

The same perimeter and a smaller area?
Perimeter = 20 units

Area = _____

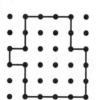

A Fascinating Fibonacci Discovery

The mathematician Fibonacci is best known for discovering the sequence that you have examined and used:

1 1 2 3 5 8 13 21 . . .

He also worked with the triangular array of numbers you see here. Using this array he developed several proofs that mathematicians still find interesting, 600 years later.

Complete this table using the array. Then write Fibonacci's discoveries from columns 3 and 4 of the table.

Row

									1	①
								3	5	②
							7	9	11	③
						13	15	17	19	④
					21	23	25	27	29	⑤
				31	33	35	37	39	41	⑥
			43	45	47	49	51	53	55	⑦
		57	59	61	63	65	67	69	71	⑧
	73	75	77	79	81	83	85	87	89	⑨
91	93	95	97	99	101	103	105	107	109	⑩

Row	Number of Terms	Sum of the Terms	Arithmetic Mean of the Terms
1	1	1	1
2	2	8	4
3	3	27	9
4	4	_____	_____
5	5	_____	_____
⋮	⋮	⋮	⋮
n	_____	_____	_____

Column 3: _____

_____

Column 4: _____

_____

Circular Sense

Try this oddity from the world of mathematics.

Write four different positive 2-digit integers in the four boxes.

Now subtract adjacent pairs, the smaller from the larger, and write the results in these four boxes.

Repeat the process and fill in these four boxes.

Continue to subtract pairs and add circles until

you notice an unusual result. What finally occurred? _____

_____

Will this work for other sets of positive integers? Must they all be 2-digit numbers? Must the first four integers all be different? Experiment with some

other sets. _____

_____

Name _____

A Bridge Problem

Königsberg, an 18th-century German town, was
built on two islands in a river and on both banks
of the river. Seven bridges connected the various
parts of the city.

People wondered whether it was possible to take a
walk around the town in such a way that each
bridge was crossed exactly one time. What do you
think they found?

Try it, following these rules:

　　Start anywhere in the city.

　　Finish anywhere in the city.

　　Cross all seven bridges, each one time only.

_____

Suppose a second bridge were built between the two

islands. Would the walk be possible then? _____